# *Establishing Healthy*
# MESSIANIC CONGREGATIONS

SAM NADLER

WORD OF MESSIAH MINISTRIES
CHARLOTTE, NC

*"Establishing Healthy Messianic Congregations: Planters, Planting, and Planning"*
*by Sam Nadler*

*Word of Messiah Ministries*

*Printed in the United States of America*
*ISBN 978-0-9786568-5-0*

# Acknowledgments

*I am thankful to all who made this book a reality:*
*Proofreading, David Taylor, Matt Nadler,*
*Sherry Nunez, Ann Thomas, and Miriam Nadler;*
*For transcribing and proofreading, Shari Belfer;*
*and Natalia Fomin, for the book layout and cover design.*
*But of course, I give all praise to Messiah, who has called me into this work*
*and allows me and these others the great privilege in His service*
*to see Messianic congregations established worldwide.*
*All to the praise of His glory!*

# CONTENTS

## Appendices: Supplemental Material



## Chart Index

# About the Author

Sam Nadler is a Jewish believer in Yeshua who has a passion to communicate the Good News and provide discipleship training for Messianic congregations. Sam plants Messianic congregations worldwide, and coaches, supports and assists congregational leaders to succeed.

Raised in New York City according to Jewish tradition, Sam hungered for what the Messiah of Israel alone can give: atonement and new life. After finding Yeshua as his Messiah in 1972, Sam has been in full-time service for Him.

Sam Nadler understands the leadership role from the inside. He was a leader in the early days of *Jews for Jesus*, beginning in 1973 through 1979. Along with his wife, Miriam, Sam pioneered the JFJ mobile evangelistic team, *The Liberated Wailing Wall*, and established JFJ's New York City branch.

In 1979, God called Sam to provide leadership for *Chosen People Ministries* (CPM). First, as CPM's NYC Director, Sam mobilized the staff to engage in team-oriented outreach, which was bold, creative, and culturally relevant. This served to enhance the ministry's local profile and evangelistic productivity.

The following year as Northeast Regional Director for CPM, Sam witnessed the Lord's blessing through an increase of staff and outreach. Convinced that the Great Commission was evangelism, which produced discipled believers, Sam began personally planting as well as supervising the planting of several Messianic congregations in the Northeast United States. As God's grace became evident, Sam was then asked to lead *Chosen People Ministries'* worldwide organization.

In 1989 as the president of CPM, Sam brought new strategic intent to the global work. With the Great Commission as his objective, Sam launched the century-old Jewish ministry in the direction of planting Messianic congregations in Jewish communities. As a result, new ministries were established in twice as many countries.

In 1996 Sam founded *Word of Messiah Ministries*, to focus on his passion and calling to provide Messianic discipleship, to develop Messianic leaders, and to plant Messianic congregations worldwide for the furtherance of the Good News. He received a doctoral degree from *Southern Evangelical Seminary* and has authored books on theology and discipleship including *Messianic Foundations*, *Messiah in the Feasts of Israel*, *The Messianic Answer Book*, *Feasts of the Bible Curriculum* and devotional commentaries on Jonah and Ruth.

## What other planters and leaders are saying about Sam's Coaching:

*The material of this book has been used in Sam Nadler's leader's coaching ministry for over 30 years. Coaching supplies a vital element for a biblically successful ministry. With coaching, a Messianic leadership team receives the mentoring and encouragement needed to navigate the maze of ministry issues, providing practical help and ongoing guidance that leaders need to accomplish their work for the Lord more effectively.*

**Michael Vowell in Calgary, Canada planting a new congregation, Mosaic:**

Despite church planting training at *Moody* and *Dallas Theological Seminary* and experience here in Canada, nothing has been able to help and guide me like Sam's coaching ministry. Let me say it another way: Sam's coaching has caused our Mosaic Fellowship to thrive, reaching new believers and making new disciples for the Messiah. Thanks to Sam's help we have set a high standard for membership and leadership which has on more than one occasion saved Mosaic from being "hijacked" by rogue elements and sifting others who were not willing to step up to our standards. What is more, in the midst of these trials my family faces constant attacks and he has been there to coach me through the emotional and spiritual trials. This is something they do not teach you in class. Lastly, Sam's encouragement as a veteran worker in the Messianic Movement is a strong motivation for my family on the mission field to keep my eyes focused on our mission and busy at efficient work. Sam has provided hands-on information, feedback, encouragement and a model that congregational planters' like myself need. God has used Sam and his coaching ministry and our congregational plant is making a measurable impact on the Jewish community of Calgary.

**Dr. Michael Herts, B'nai Avraham Messianic Fellowship, Hampton, VA**

Dr. Sam Nadler with *Word of Messiah Ministries* has been the most instrumental of all the resources available to me as a congregation planter. His consistent mentoring took us from a God-given calling to a congregation about to be fully birthed. His focus on evangelism and disciple making, affirming a statement of faith, and developing a set of values that guide a congregation has saved us from many of the pitfalls that other congregational plants face. His individual mentoring, prayer, and encouragement has kept me on track when challenges seemed overwhelming. *B'nai Avraham Messianic Fellowship* would not be successful today if we did not have his guidance. I look forward to calling on his wisdom and experience in the future as we manage the many challenges of a growing congregation.

**Jeffrey Dumont, Lion of Judah Messianic Fellowship, leading a new congregation plant in Georgia**

I want to say thank you for the lessons I'm learning in your video series of developing the congregation. I am sending it to our core group and wait to hear from them. I'm so excited to have the opportunity to learn what I need to know, even if I thought I knew it already. Thank you for this work you've put together. For anyone preparing to plant a congregation, this is a must see and I wish I would have had it four years ago when we hit the ground running and found several potholes in the road.

**Larry Rose, elder of Eitz Chaim, an established congregation in Dallas, Texas**

We are pleased to report that your work at *Eitz Chaim* has produced fruit. Our discipleship program will utilize your Messianic Discipleship book. Much has happened since you were here, mainly through the work of the Spirit that opened a dialogue within leadership to re-think our focus and vision. We are presently revamping our services, activities and printed materials to reflect a clearer focus on the Gospel. I cannot adequately express our appreciation for your work here, and how instrumental you were in our decisions. We had a visitor accept Yeshua last Shabbat, which was the first saved in many years; we believe it is evidence of the first fruit from the seeds you planted.

**Scott Brown, former leader of Messianic congregation Son of David in Rockville, Maryland**

Sam was the first to give me what I really needed. He rifled solutions to me, which advanced me toward my goal. By God's grace, Sam Nadler's coaching made the difference between success and failure in my ministry.

**Vladimir Pikman, Messianic congregation leader in Berlin, Germany**

Sam's leadership training and coaching helped me to have better priorities for my family and ministry. I now understand and am able to accomplish the Great Commission in a more effective, wise, and comprehensive manner.

**Jonathan Sacks, congregation leader of Beth Sar Shalom Congregation in Bowling Green, KY**

Over the past several years, the Lord has used Sam Nadler to help us identify and implement congregational systems that have helped us minister more effectively. Implementing, reviewing, and modifying systems for making contacts, disciples, members, and leaders is essential for to fulfill its calling and vision to be fruitful in making disciples in our area and beyond.

# Forward

I wrote this book because there is a need to have more sound and functional Messianic congregations that effectively testify that Yeshua is the faithfulness of God to both Israel and the nations. It is my desire and goal for "all Israel to be saved," that is, for the Jewish people as a whole to come to personal faith in Messiah Yeshua (Romans 10:1; 11:26).

In Jeremiah 31:35-37 God has made a gracious commitment to preserve the Jewish people as an identifiable nation:

> Thus says the Lord, Who gives the sun for light by day, and the fixed order of the moon and the stars for light by night, Who stirs up the sea so that its waves roar; The Lord of hosts is His name; "If this fixed order departs from before Me," declares the Lord, "then the offspring of Israel also will cease from being a nation forever." Thus says the Lord, "If the heavens above can be measured and the foundations of the earth searched out below, then I will also cast off all the offspring of Israel for all that they have done," declares the Lord.

A Messianic congregation is an expression of God's gracious commitment and is essential to His Great Commission (Matthew 28:18-20). Yeshua has "all the authority in heaven and on earth," and with that authority He has commanded us to make disciples (Matthew 28:18). If we are convinced of His Lordship, we must therefore be committed to His discipleship, for He said, "Go, therefore and make disciples of all nations" (Matthew 28:19). This means raising new believers in the faith so that they will live out God's faithfulness in their circumstances.

It starts with immersion, which testifies publicly to what the Spirit did at salvation, identifying the new believer with the Lord (Matthew 28:20). However, discipleship is not only the one time act of immersion but it is the ongoing activity of growing as believers in all that Yeshua has commanded. We are to teach the truth, not merely transfer information, so that believers will observe, or do, all that Yeshua commanded.

The primary function of any congregation is as a disciple-making center, even as the Lord's faithfulness is fully seen in a discipled believer. If a new believer understands his or her Jewish identity in Messiah, then this same God who promised that He would not "leave nor forsake our people" is seen in the eyes of the Jewish community, and to all who are looking, as the same faithful Lord who said, "I am with you always to the end of the age" (Joshua 1:9; Matthew 28:20). Also, as Gentiles are saved through the evangelistic work of Messianic congregations they will be grounded and grow in the same faith, by the same discipleship. This makes their own communication of the Good News more clear and meaningful to the Jewish people and all people. This is how Gentile believers are "to make Israel jealous" (Romans 11:11) and fulfill their calling in the Good News. The Olive Tree, even with wild branches in abundance is God's testimony of His ongoing faithfulness to the Jewish people. Despite all that the enemy has attempted to do, the Jewish people have been kept by God and that in Messiah, we, as a remnant people, are restored to God's service and testimony. The existence of Messianic congregations testifies to God's triumph.

We are blessed to live in such a time where we see Messianic congregations springing up in the last century as part of the renewal of the Jewish testimony to Yeshua. As such, they are centers for worship, instruction, fellowship, and proclaiming the Good News of Messiah. But ... what does it take to get one started? What does a healthy Messianic congregation actually do? How in their activities do they glorify Messiah? What is required to be called a congregation? This book is written to present just that information.

It is easy to focus on externals and surface matters, but in reality Messianic congregations are manifestations of God's calling in the world. All who are called by the name of Messiah are called to help build up the local congregation. Here is a practical guide to planting and establishing of healthy communities which proclaim God's faithfulness to Israel and the nations.

I have learned from planting congregations that certain basic responsibilities and systems are vital to a functional Messianic congregation. My prayer and hope is that this guide will prove to be beneficial in your labor of planting and leading a Messianic congregation.

Sam Nadler

November 15, 2011

# Debunking the Myths

From my experience, there are many misunderstandings that hinder the work of Messiah. Here are a few myths that I hope to debunk so that your path may be a bit clearer as you move ahead with Adonai.

### *Myth 1: "I am a congregation if I say so."*

Often, what is called a Messianic congregation is actually a Bible study. Not knowing what a congregation is can lead a person to call anything that has Messianic expression of faith a congregation. Now, it is not the size of the group that makes it a congregation, but it is a matter of the mutual commitment and loving accountability in Messiah (Hebrews 10:24-25). A congregation has a four-fold work which can be described with the acrostic WIFE: Worship Center, Instruction Center, Fellowship Center, Evangelism Center. Being a "center" for these things implies a rootedness of commitment and accountability which is not found in other groupings.

### *Myth 2: "Messianic congregations shouldn't do evangelism."*

Regrettably, it is true that many Messianic synagogues, or even churches for that matter, do not share their faith. This indicates a spiritual weakness and disobedience, because we are under a mandate to proclaim the Good News. Evangelism needs to be in the DNA of the group. Even with just a small core group, which is the start-up for a congregation, the leadership is to teach and equip them to personally witness, and be inviting pre-believers to services, etc.

### *Myth 3: "Our service needs be centered on the Torah to be messianic."*

It is true that traditional Orthodox services are Torah-centered. Everything in the service is either before or after the Torah is read. It is also true that Messianic congregations faithfully utilize Moses to proclaim Messiah, for it speaks of Him (John 5:39). However, with the use of Torah, Messianic congregations must be Yeshua-centered, for Messiah is the very substance of all that we do – our worship is in His name or it is false worship. Apart from Him we can do nothing.

### *Myth 4: "Messianic congregations are under the Mosaic Covenant."*

Since we utilize the Torah of Moses as well as all of the Tanakh to express all aspects of our faith, some may think that this means we're under the jurisdiction, or rule, of the Mosaic Covenant. However, we must be under the authority of the New Covenant. For example, Yeshua cannot intercede for us as High Priest through the Torah of Moses; He does not even qualify to be such a priest under the Torah (see Hebrews 7 - 8). It is because of the New Covenant that we are truly saved and have the benefits of His ministry. The New Covenant is the flowering of the Torah and Hebrew Scriptures. As Messianic congregations we apply all of the Tanakh by the New Covenant's authority and purpose (1 Timothy 1:9-11; 2 Timothy 3:16).

### *Myth 5: "Legitimate Messianic congregation have Jewish majorities."*

In some Messianic communities with a majority of Gentile believers, there could be a sense of a lack of validation. The truth is that every Messianic congregation needs to win everyone in their community to Yeshua, Jew and Gentile alike. Since most of the world's population is Gentile, an effective Messianic congregation should actually expect to include many Gentile believers. What is vital is that these Gentile believers are discipled properly, so that they will express their faith in a way that testifies to the greater Jewish community. The Good News, claiming "to the Jew first," shows its value to both Jews and Gentiles.

### *Myth 6: "Messianic Gentiles are Jewish wannabe's."*

Certainly, God loves Gentiles and Jews equally (John 3:16), and does not want Gentiles to become Jews any more than He wants Jews to become Gentiles. In fact, God's plan for Gentiles to express their faith in Messiah proves His faithfulness to Israel (Romans 11:11). Gentiles demonstrate that Yeshua is the true Messiah of Israel and therefore Savior of the world, for in Yeshua all the nations will be blessed (Genesis 12:3; Galatians 3:8). Rather, by practicing the faith with an expression sensible to Jewish people, they are not seeking to become Jews, but are testifying to the blessings only found in Messiah of Israel (Colossians 2:10; Ephesians 1:3).

### *Myth 7: "Messianic Congregations must be led by Messianic Jews."*

Because of this myth, some congregations have overlooked qualified Gentile believers and "laid hands on" some not so qualified Jewish believers. However, being a Gentile believer doesn't invalidate you as an effective Messianic leader any more than being a Jewish believer validates you as an effective leader—figure head, maybe; leader, not so much. In all Messianic congregations both Jewish and Gentile believers should be equally discipled in Messianic values, such that, as they mature, they will properly take their place in Messianic leadership, even as congregational leader of a Messianic synagogue. We need Messianic Gentile leaders like Luke and Titus as well as Messianic Jewish leaders like Paul and Timothy to lead Messianic congregations and the Messianic movement for the glory of HaShem.

# PART 1

# THE MESSIANIC CONGREGATIONAL PLANTER

## Chapter 1

# Congregation Planter And Core Group

Has God called you to plant a Messianic congregation? Though God calls all believers to serve Him, some are called to plant and lead Messianic congregations. To be called to plant a Messianic congregation is not only a great calling but also a great responsibility. However, calling is not enough to do God's work. There are several vital matters the congregational leader needs to consider in his preparation to plant a congregation. These may be matters which are already quite established in your life; however, it wouldn't hurt to double check by making of an inventory of these basic matters which we must all integrate into our lives.

Some of these vital matters should include: prayer, accountability, marital unity, vision, sound teaching, biblical calendar, awareness of culture, and adequate time. In the following pages we will take a brief look at each of these matters as they apply to the daily life of a planter.

## Prayer

The first matter is prayer. This is very important for the planter, but even more for his team (which may or may not exist yet). Ultimately, a congregation is a work of God Himself, expressing a community's encounter with Him. The leader must not only be in prayer but also have others pray for him. He should develop prayer-supportive teams to assist, to stand alongside, and to undergird the work of planting as it moves forward.

The importance of prayer in our service is illustrated in Israel's first battle when they came out of Egypt. Joshua may have led the fighting of the Amalekites with the Israeli army, but Moses was standing on the top of the mountain with his arms outstretched to God. The activity of prayer was the key to Israel's victory.

> Now Amalek came and fought with Israel in Rephidim. And Moses said to Joshua, "Choose us some men and go out, fight with Amalek. Tomorrow I will stand on the top of the hill with the rod of God in my hand." So Joshua did as Moses said to him, and fought with Amalek. And Moses, Aaron, and Hur went up to the top of the hill. And so it was, when Moses held up his hand, that Israel prevailed; and when he let down his hand, Amalek prevailed. But Moses' hands became heavy; so they took a stone and put it under him, and he sat on it. And Aaron and Hur supported his hands, one on one side, and the other on the other side; and his hands were steady until the going down of the sun. So Joshua defeated Amalek and his people with the edge of the sword. Then the LORD said to Moses, "Write this for a memorial in the book and recount it in the hearing of Joshua, that I will utterly blot out the remembrance of Amalek from under heaven." And Moses built an altar and called its name, The-LORD-Is-My-Banner; for he said, "Because the LORD has sworn: the LORD will have war with Amalek from generation to generation. (Exodus 17:8-16)

Therefore, prayer is the key to victory for the planter who is involved in planting Messianic congregations.

## ACCOUNTABILITY

Planters tend to be entrepreneurial pioneers; however, this does not diminish the essential need for accountability. Accountability may be available if the planter is part of a larger network or organization which is already involved in planting congregations. If, however, he finds himself unassociated with a particular network, it is vital to seek out mentorship. It may even be good for a planter to have several mentors. I suggest five qualities to look for in a mentor:

1. Experience, providing sound counsel
2. Personal love and concern
3. Objectivity
4. Proven character
5. Not controlling, but rather always seeking what is best for the planter.

## MARITAL UNITY

Another essential matter is marital unity. Of course, being single does not disqualify one from becoming a planter. However, those who are married must have marital unity. One's spouse should be committed to the work as a calling. The children must also be taken into consideration. For example, the planter may need to pioneer a children's ministry, which might involve only his own children for a time. The family takes priority over the congregation.

## CLEAR VISION

The greatest vision is to proclaim the Good News of Yeshua. We look to Him alone as we run the race set before us (Hebrews 12:1). That being stated, the planter must have a clear vision and conviction as to why Messianic congregations must exist. This is the primary focus of this book. A clear vision and steady values will reflect biblical truth.

## SOUND TEACHING

The key for a sound congregation, and what the congregation will be planted upon, is the Word of God. Healthy teaching is always focused on Yeshua, and whatever distracts us from Him, as Paul warns, is a "doctrine of demons" (1 Timothy 3:16-4:1). Therefore, sound biblical teaching is the foundation of your work as a planter.

NOTES:

## BIBLICAL CALENDAR

The planter should understand his calendar. The schedule of a congregation through the year is based upon the biblical calendar and the feasts of Israel.

### PLANNING AROUND THE FESTIVALS

The *mo'adim* are the calendar markers for the yearly congregational planning process. The feasts ought to be observed with Yeshua at their spiritual center, because of what Yeshua Himself teaches (John 5:39). Still, there is wide room for discussion on how to observe the feasts. The New Covenant gives little information on how the first century believers celebrated the feasts. Paul's instructions to the Corinthians tell us, for the believers Messiah was central to Passover (1 Corinthians 5:6-7). Even in what might have been a predominantly Gentile congregation as in Corinth, Paul still taught them to "keep the feast" (1 Corinthians 5:8). Even so, for many congregations being able to celebrate on the exact day of the feast is not always easy. For example, facilities, which are rented for a Shabbat morning service, may not be available for a Wednesday evening

Rosh Hashanah service. To accommodate this issue, sometimes the week of the festival can be marked by a special observance or teaching on Shabbat, or there can be a "Preparing for Yom Kippur" service. Therefore, I do not insist that congregations make a priority of observing any biblical feast on precise dates, since it may appear that the celebrations are more about the congregation being right in its externals rather than testifying of Messiah (Colossians 3:16-17). Since a spiritually healthy Messianic congregation understands evangelism, the service should be organized as outreach as well as community worship. This gives everyone an opportunity to invite relatives, neighbors, co-workers, fellow students, etc., to hear the Good News in connection to these days, which are both biblical and a part of the life of Jewish people. Let's consider the seasons in a brief overview.

## SPRINGTIME AND SUMMER

Passover begins the annual calendar of redemption. As mentioned above, the feasts of Israel provide outreach opportunities to the community both at a congregational level and a family level. First, the congregation can give instruction where necessary on how the community observes the festivals. For example, removal of leaven from the home prior to the Passover observance, and on the Shabbat with in Passover week, it should be certain there is no leaven at the oneg, and of course, provide the teaching on the cleansing of our souls before HaShem, the Messiah, the Passover Lamb.

Second, most congregations organize a Passover Seder which provides a high profile outreach to the larger community. In addition, immediately following the Passover and feast of Unleavened Bread is *Reishit*, or the feast of First Fruits. Besides counting the *Omer* as many communities do, this is also a great time to speak about the resurrection of Messiah (1 Corinthians 15:20). Counting the *Omer* is a traditional observance from the command "you shall count." This time lends itself to fifty days of prayer, Bible reading, witnessing and many other edifying opportunities for the new congregation.

*Shavuot*, which is traditionally a dairy *oneg*, is a time that we recognize the Torah being given at Mount Sinai, and so it is called, "The Season of the Giving of the Law." Since its fulfillment is in the giving of the Holy Spirit (Acts 2:1), it also lends itself to teaching the work of *Ruach HaKodesh*, and our unity in the Body of Messiah.

## AUTUMN AND WINTER

The Fall Feasts are in some ways best known by the traditions that clothe them. For example, *Zikhron Teruah* (reminder of blowing of trumpets, Leviticus

NOTES:

23:24) is certainly better known as Rosh Hashanah. Therefore, teaching on the last shofar, which seems to be Paul's focus (1 Corinthians 15:51-52), is one way to keep us all ready for our blessed hope (Titus 2:13). Rosh Hashanah is traditionally called *Yom HaDin*, or Judgment Day and gives an opportunity to teach the truth of our names being written in the Book of Life, not just for the coming year, but also for eternity.

The observance of *Yom Kippur* provides us with worship and witness through a solemn assembly and a fast day (Act 27:9). We are to mourn with those who mourn, even with the greater Jewish community, who fast on this day without recognizing the atonement which Yeshua provides. People should be informed not to bring food or drinks into the service. It should also be understood, that small children and the frail should not fast, and people should continue to take their medications. It is appropriate to teach on the necessity of blood atonement, and that repentance and fasting are customary expressions of faith in that atonement.

*Sukkot* is a time of rejoicing and fun for the congregation and the families of the community. If space is available, building a *sukkah* (booth) and decorating it together can be a community project. For the first seven days of *Sukkot*, worship services should be celebratory. Since *lulavs* and *etrogs* are essential elements of celebration, but may not be available for every individual to have one, Scripture permits the use of other branches (Nehemiah 8:15). *Sukkot* testifies of His provision and protection as it points to Yeshua (John 1:14; Romans 8:1; Colossians 2:9-10; Revelation 7:9-17).

NOTES:

Many more occasions in addition to the *mo'adim* of Leviticus 23 present opportunities to testify of His glory and grace. *Simchat Torah,* though a traditional addition to the calendar, is a great reminder that His Word is not only authoritative, but also a cause for real celebration. The drama and rejoicing of Purim, as well as the solemnity of Holocaust Remembrance Day, are both poignant reminders, which despite the Hamans and Hitlers, His promises keep His people and all who will trust in the Lord.

*Hanukkah* (John 10:22) is a yearly reminder that HaShem can only be glorified in a cleansed temple, and as such we are bought with a price. Families may be encouraged to celebrate both Hanukkah and Purim at home.

In this way we plan out the year to orient our congregations around His great theme of redemption, in Messiah Yeshua, as a demonstration of His promises to the Jew first, but not to the Jew only (Romans 1:16).

## CULTURE

The planter must understand the culture of the community in which he will plant. It is common knowledge that no two Jewish communities are perfectly alike. As it has been said, "three Jews, five opinions." The congregations need to adjust to the surrounding greater Jewish community in order to effectively communicate the Good News. Better understanding of the community, will bring about more effective communication. It is helpful to know the jargon of the community you are working in. For example, a Sephardic community may or may not speak Spanish, an Ashkenazi community may or may not speak Yiddish, and if it is a secular or largely assimilated community you will want to be aware of that, and sensitive to this fact as well. In general, one should get to know the area and neighborhood. If you are in the downtown area of the city, you may find parking can be an issue. Also, in a residential area you may find public transportation is not readily available. Know the kind of area you are working in.

## ADEQUATE TIME

Finally, consider the time it takes to plant a healthy congregation. We know weeds grow fast, but fruit trees take a while to produce fruit. The fruit tree requires time to mature. In fact, the Torah teaches a newly planted tree's fruit could not be harvested and eaten for several years (Leviticus 19:23). This principle may be applied to planting a Messianic congregation, as it takes time to develop and mature.

In the next section we overview a variety of methods as to how congregations may be planted.

## A PLANTER'S METHODOLOGY

There's more than one way to plant a Messianic congregation. These particular strategies will depend on prayerful consideration, the organization behind it, and the resources available.

### PIONEERING

The first method, which is most commonly used, is called pioneering. A planter goes into an area and begins gathering a core group through evangelism or making contacts. This is usually necessary in new areas where there are no other Messianic congregation partners to assist a planter. For example, *Hope of Israel Congregation* in Charlotte, North Carolina was planted utilizing this method.

NOTES:

### BRANCHING

Another approach is called branching. In this method, a core group "hives off" from a parent congregation, while staying in the same general vicinity. This method provides a core group with developed values and relationships and can easily find a support system from the parent congregation nearby. The value in branching is that the people already having known each other will also understand the values involved. They may share the same beliefs and practices which are important to a congregation, and there may be less time needed for core group development. *Shoresh David Messianic Synagogue* in Lakeland, Florida, is an example of this.

### COLONIZING

Colonizing happens when members of one congregation form a core group and intentionally relocate from the parent congregation to plant in a completely different area. This provides the developed core group, but it does not provide the support system of a nearby parent congregation. Therefore, the people involved will be tightly knit and know each other. The trust and unity they have in Yeshua is the basis for the community.

### SEEDING

Seeding is a situation where you have key leaders that may, because of a job or other reasons, relocate from the area they are currently in and develop a core group in a new area, which leads to forming a new community. This could be with just a few families who move together to a new area. Obviously there would be a strong bond within these families as well.

NOTES:

### ADOPTING

Another approach is adoption. A core group or fellowship may approach an established group for resources. The established congregation then embraces and sponsors the fledgling group. Some denominations utilize this method, for example, congregations of the *Southern Baptist Messianic Fellowship* (SBMF) are involved in this type of approach as part of the North American Mission Board (NAMB).

### PARTNERING

Partnering is where several smaller groups may work cooperatively to venture out and start a new congregation. An historic example of this approach is the *Jerusalem Assembly*, which in the 1960s began as four Bible studies combined to form one congregation.

### REVITALIZING

When a congregation is not doing well, flickering, or on its last legs, a new work may really mean revitalization, or a restart of an old work. This may be done through new leadership or a different approach in the community. Revitalizing is difficult; as is often said, it is easier to give birth to babies than to raise the dead. It is, however, one approach.

### TRANSPLANTING

Transplanting is the inverse of revitalizing. Here, a congregation and its membership relocate to start one or possibly several new congregations. This was sometimes seen in the phenomenon known as "white flight." In many cities, the community changes its ethnic demographics and the congregation wants to move on. Regardless of cause, the result can nonetheless be helpful to the work of God as well.

### CATALYZING

This is where a dynamic, vision-casting Messianic leader sparks the start of many congregations as he casts the vision in many different communities. This is sometimes considered "apostolic," but in reality catalyzing is a part of what many missionaries do.

It is crucially important to consider which of these approaches is being utilized. Each may entail its own considerations and strategies. For example, the case of branching is not a disgruntled group splitting off from a congregation. Rather, starting new congregations should be part of the strategic work of the parent congregation. This implies that some of the members leave with the blessing of the leadership to start a congregation in a nearby community. The leadership of the parent congregation must already have the vision for new work to begin so people do not see themselves as needing to divide their community.

## QUALITIES OF THE PLANTER AND HIS CORE GROUP

To plant a Messianic congregation takes more than one talented leader. Although called by God to do the work of reaching out to Jewish people and building a testimony in the community, there is a need to develop and form a core group. There are a number of qualities that are necessary for successful congregation planting. In this section we will look at each quality including: faith-vision, faithfulness, vision casting, ready witness, self-starter, couple-power, resourcefulness, resilience, redemptiveness, goal-orientation, multiplier,

NOTES:

and flexibility. This list might look overwhelming and even intimidating, however, these qualities are found in individuals that make up your core group. The qualities combined by the core group will always surpass the one individual who brings many qualities to the table. One person could contribute in a big way by possessing at least one of these qualities. All these qualities are found in the Scriptures.

## FAITH-VISION

> Now faith is the assurance of things hoped for, the conviction of things not seen. (Hebrews 11:1)

The first quality is faith. A person of faith sees what is not there (yet). Since faith is the very essence and the proof of the planter's calling, he believes God for all things. The person of faith will take risks. To plant a Messianic congregation means to venture out "into the water" (Joshua 3:8).

I recall at the very early stages of planting a congregation, we had a division in the core-group which threatened its existence. In the midst of this trial, I was discipling a new believer, Rich. It was Friday evening. *Erev Shabbat* service was to begin in a few minutes, and only Rich and I were there. He asked, "Sam, what will you do if no one comes back?" "Rich, we will start again, because I believe that the Lord wants a Messianic congregation here".

NOTES:

Though these matters weighed heavily on me, I believed the Lord wanted a Messianic congregation established. Eventually, healing and unity was restored in the group, and we moved forward. Nonetheless, such challenges are typical, and a man of faith is needed to meet them.

A planter is not, however, to be imprudent. Faith may be bold but not rash and foolish. A planter sees *what* God wants to see accomplished and trusts the Lord to provide for *how* it will be accomplished.

## FAITHFULNESS

> In this case, moreover, it is required of stewards that one be found trustworthy. (1 Corinthians 4:2)

Faithfulness speaks of the character of the individual, as well as the integrity of the person. A faithful person models the faith and is seen as a standard bearer for honoring the Lord. In giving the qualifications for elders, 1 Timothy 5 explains, "For if a man does not know how to manage his own home, how will he manage the assembly of God?" The values of faithfulness need to be seen in the home which will be reproduced in the community and the congregation.

I was thankful to learn the Lord does not call the qualified but rather qualifies the called. Quite often I felt ill-prepared for the challenges I faced both in experience and developed skills. But I learned early on, my faithful reliance upon the Lord would provide the very fruit He desired. It wasn't unusual for me to come home totally exhausted from the daily activities; nevertheless, I knew my family needed a dad and husband. I just did not have the resources to give. I learned, before putting my key in the door, to pray and ask for His empowerment.

A planter should seek to keep his commitments (Psalm 15:4); this is required of a servant. We are to be found faithful (1 Corinthians 4:2), and we are faithful by abiding in Messiah (John 15:5).

## VISION CASTING

> Where there is no vision, the people are unrestrained, but happy is he who keeps the law. (Proverbs 29:18)

Another quality is vision casting, which is the ability to communicate the vision for a Messianic congregation to others. According to Proverbs 29:18, "Without vision the people perish," that is, they are in disarray. Vision gives focus and clarity, a sense of direction, so others have the opportunity to join in and accomplish the goals. Casting a vision brings clarity of thought and helps create ownership of the mission, thereby building cohesiveness. That same verse concludes, "But happy is he who keeps the Torah"—this is where we acquire our lasting vision and where we can thereby renew our focus for service.

We also need to orient our focus on the primary importance of following Messiah. Sometimes inconveniences and diversions distract and diffuse our focus. Therefore, the planter's responsibility is to keep the team's focus on the mission and vision, and if needed, refocus them towards the goal.

## READY WITNESS

Some of us are not naturally bold, but we need to develop into a ready witness, one who purposely reaches out with the Good News. Proverbs 11:30 says, "He who wins souls is wise." We need to know how to relate to those who do not know the Lord, reach out to outsiders and think of them as pre-believers with a vision and hope for their lives to be fulfilled in the Messiah.

Therefore, it is important to be friendly and be able to interact with others, because some opportunities to share are planned and others unexpected. When I travel, I assume the people sitting next to me on planes are ordained to hear the Good News.

NOTES:

Evangelism may not be everyone's gift; however, it is everyone's responsibility and an important part of the work to which God has called us.

## SELF-STARTER

> Poor is he who works with a negligent hand, but the hand of the diligent makes rich. (Proverbs 10:4)

Accountability is essential, yet being a self-starter is equally important. In some cases, a congregational planter will not have a human boss to report to about his work, only to the Lord alone. Indeed, the Holy Spirit encourages and motivates the planter to serve and do his work faithfully. The planter's intrinsic motivation is for service, focusing on doing what needs to get done and motivated by the Spirit's desire to accomplish the will of God. Relying on the Holy Spirit to lead him, he will take the initiative in faithfulness; to his family, discipline in prayer, the Word, as well as in reaching out to others.

## COUPLE POWER

> You husbands in the same way, live with your wives in an understanding way, as with someone weaker, since she is a woman; and show her honor as a fellow heir of the grace of life, so that your prayers will not be hindered. (1 Peter 3:7)

NOTES:

Peter warns us that our prayers can go unanswered. The unity of a husband and wife cannot be understated. Marriage always comes first and must be valued before congregational work since the work of the congregation is an outworking of the home (1 Timothy 3:5). If one's spouse is not prepared to assist with the planting of a congregation, it may not be the timing of the Lord to get started. However, as one's wife supports the ministry, they can face issues and difficulties in the work together. The planter will utilize her gifts in the ministry of the congregation. Valuing and empowering one's spouse evidences the very values of the congregation.

I had one leader wait three years before venturing out into planting a congregation until his wife was in full agreement for this ministry. On another occasion, I counseled another planter to remove a valued person from his core-group because the person's spouse was against being a part of the Messianic congregation. The planter has to demonstrate his commitment to families; a congregation is only as strong as its families. There is blessed power in couple-power (Genesis 1:28) when it comes to planting and leading a Messianic congregation.

## RESOURCEFULNESS

The planter and his team should know how to improvise. We can learn from Yeshua's resourcefulness. In Matthew 13:2, we read how Yeshua used a boat as His pulpit when He taught. A planter knows how to utilize what is available, which involves being aware of the existing opportunities in the community.

In pioneering a work, we use what is available for the sake of the Good News. Let me share a personal example. In a congregation I planted in Connecticut, the person responsible for the worship music couldn't make it to the service. To redeem the situation, I found a hand drum and led in a few simple praise songs. Consequently, a number of people volunteered to replace me on the spot; but the service continued without major difficulty. We need to be ready to come up with solutions on the spot. Therefore, resourcefulness is a necessary quality.

## REDEMPTIVENESS

> Walk in wisdom toward those who are outside, redeeming the time. (Colossians 4:5)

> See then that you walk circumspectly, not as fools but as wise, redeeming the time, because the days are evil. (Ephesians 5:15-16)

> For while I was passing through and examining the objects of your worship, I also found an altar with this inscription, 'TO AN UNKNOWN GOD.' Therefore what you worship in ignorance, this I proclaim to you. (Acts 17:23)

NOTES:

Along with being resourceful, we also need to be redeeming in our approach. A community is full of opportunities. A planter and his team must be creative and responsive to the community. Understanding the community, they are able to utilize its distinctiveness. For example, if you minister among a very Orthodox community, the application will be more traditional, whereas the opportunities might not be the same in a very secular community. As Paul used his Roman citizenship, so we too utilize all that is available and all that we have for the sake of the Good News and the planting of a Messianic congregation. We are under a mandate to redeem the time and the available opportunities.

## RESILIENCE

> Hatred stirs up strife, but love covers all transgressions. (Proverbs 10:12)

> Above all, keep fervent in your love for one another, because love covers a multitude of sins. (1 Peter 4:8)

A planter and his team need to be resilient. At times, it means to have a forehead like a flint (Ezekiel 3:9), to be able to "take a punch," so to speak, and not be easily offended. We are to be caring and gentle even to the least of the brethren, yet this does not mean to be fragile. We need to be more shock absorbers than shock emitters.

As it has been said, there are a lot of bumps and potholes on the highway to holiness. The planter has to be able to deal with problems as they come up. You have to be focused on what God has called you to do and not be easily discouraged.

### GOAL-ORIENTATION

> Brethren, I do not regard myself as having laid hold of it yet; but one thing I do: forgetting what lies behind and reaching forward to what lies ahead, I press on toward the goal for the prize of the upward call of God in Messiah Yeshua. (Philippians 3:13-14)

"One thing I do," said Paul, in Philippians 3:13. Like Paul we must be focused on the primary issues of the work of God. We must learn to see the minor issues for what they are and never let them take the focus off the major issues, which are compelling for life. This keeps the vision alive, and the team dedicated and encouraged. The planter and his team are strategic in their planning, being oriented towards the finish line in what God has called the team to accomplish.

NOTES:

### MULTIPLIER

> Go therefore and make disciples of all the nations, baptizing them in the name of the Father and the Son and the Holy Spirit. (Matthew 28:19)

A lot of planters, because they are pioneers, are accustomed to doing everything themselves. A good planter understands the congregation will develop and be established as people take ownership. This builds cohesiveness in the body as we share the vision, values and service, focusing on Messiah and His work. A planter responds to the command to make *talmidim* (disciples) by motivating others to get involved, delegating responsibilities and keeping things on track. He empowers individuals and does not control all the information or authority. He is looking to develop an empowered community.

### FLEXIBILITY

> Come now, you who say, "Today or tomorrow we will go to such and such a city, and spend a year there and engage in business and make a profit." (James 4:13)

Flexibility is vital in congregational work. In reality, things don't always go smoothly. In fact, I have found that very little works out! One has to be flexible, trying different approaches and different strategies in order to accomplish the goal of congregation planting. At times, the key people you hoped would join you do not become part of the core group. You have to be flexible and move on and get other people involved. All the assumptions of what you want to see accomplished should be in the hands of God (James 4:15). Seek His will, His power, and His calling.

Though principles remain the same, flexibility may require becoming cross-cultural. The individual planter may have his own preferences, which may reflect the community he came from, or may even be reacting to what he did not like in that community. However, the planter needs to learn what is customary to the community he is reaching (1 Corinthians 9:20-21). You have to focus on what you need to get done, and be flexible on how you get there.

These are qualifications, which are needed in a planter and a core group. Remember, the planter may not be strong in all of these areas, however God will raise up a group of people, which are able to do great and mighty things. As the vision is cast, it points us to Yeshua. He will help us meet the challenges as we look to Him.

## Chapter 2

# Vision of a Planter

In Acts 16, the Holy Spirit hindered Paul from doing any further work in Asia Minor. Then the Lord gave Paul a vision of a man from Macedonia who was beseeching him to come and bring the Good News to Macedonia. This vision shifted his ministry focus, and opened a new door into Europe. God can also rearrange our plans and give us new vision.

A true vision comes from the Lord. He places a burden on His servants of what He wants to accomplish (Nehemiah 2:12). Nehemiah was an administrator seeking the Lord as he was burdened for his people. While in prayer the Lord gave him a vision for a work to be done in Jerusalem, to rebuild the wall. Today is no different, God calls servants to represent His redemptive work among the Jewish people and gives a vision to plant and establish Messianic congregations in Jewish communities, which would testify to His unfailing love and eternal commitment to His people.

One might ask, what is a vision? A vision is a future and potential reality of what may be achieved. How one receives vision may vary, whether from Scripture you read, a speaker you heard, or a trying experience. Ultimately, it is the Lord who places the vision in our hearts.

To plant a flourishing congregation there needs to be unifying vision which keeps our focus on the work that needs to be accomplished. Three things must be noted:

1. A vision helps us to understand what God calls us to do, to accomplish His will for His glory.

2. A vision necessitates fulfillment through the congregation. A vision from God is always greater than what the individual can accomplish on his or her own. It is not about what I do, but what we do as Messiah leads us through the unified vision.

3. A vision is always going to be dependent upon grace, requiring that we have faith. A vision from God has to do with His grace proving to be sufficient. We each may know our own strengths and weaknesses to some degree; however, God is not dependent upon our strengths or limited by our weaknesses. God encouraged Paul in his struggles, "My grace is sufficient for you, for My strength is made perfect in weakness" (2 Corinthians 12:9).

Our calling depends upon His grace for fulfillment, whether it is to start a family or start a congregation. The purpose of a vision is to give unity to the congregation and to remind us that we depend upon His grace for fulfillment of the vision, as we trust in Him by faith in Messiah Yeshua.

The vision which God has called us to accomplish is beyond our present victories, and, therefore, beyond our present wisdom. Perhaps the very victories we are presently enjoying are a result of wisdom gained through past situations. God calls us to do something new, especially when it comes to planting congregations. Therefore, we need to be prepared to see things differently and adapt to the community we serve, since every congregation and every community will be different. Ultimately, the vision of a Messianic congregation reveals God's character. The congregation is in essence a community of people, the body of Messiah. In our love for each other, we evidence the very character of God. After all, it is not merely a work to be done, but the life of Yeshua to be lived out.

## HINDRANCES TO VISION

I was invited to assist in a new Messianic congregation plant in the Midwest United States. I found the leadership of the core group consisting of five leaders in disarray because they were not sure how to proceed with God's work. I asked each leader to individually give me their vision for their congregation. I heard five different answers as to what they thought the vision was. One said, we want to teach Hebraic roots, another said evangelism, yet another thought they were to keep Torah, etc. I told them a unified vision has to be established, because if they succeeded in any one of the "visions" mentioned, there would be four others, who would be very disappointed people! In other words, they did not have a unified vision, which was the root of their problem. A unifying vision for the congregation is essential. "Without vision the people are in disarray" (Proverbs 29:18).

If a unifying vision is needed, then we want to consider the matters that hinder such a unifying vision. In my experience I found the most common hindrances to unifying vision are: fear, stereotyping, fatigue, short-term thinking, unqualified leadership, and tradition. Let us take a quick overview of each of them and perhaps you can see if any of these apply to your situation.

## FEAR

One common hindrance to unifying vision is fear. We are called to be people of faith. Life is filled with difficulties, trials, and problems, but God is greater than any problem we might face. David could stand up to a Goliath, not because he minimized the problem, but because he knew the Lord, who was bigger than the problem.

Fear may find a place in your heart when you are pioneering a work in a new community. Therefore, you will want to be wise, not fearful. Have courage to embrace support from the believing community and ask for their prayers, and treasure their encouragement. Instead of being fearful, build relationships.

## STEREOTYPING

NOTES:

Be careful of limiting the work of God by stereotyping. God's grace is sufficient for any person. It is easy to limit leadership and service to a particular personality profile; however we should rely on how God views individuals rather than on people's perceptions. According to the Scriptures, I am not who people say I am, not even who I say I am, but rather, I am who God says I am. Hence, I'm a child of God. My circumstances and personality do not limit me. In Messiah, I have all the needed resources to fulfill His will, and I am more than a conqueror through Him who loves me (Romans 8:37).

Getting rid of our stereotypes means trusting the Lord to work through whomever He pleases. God used a Jewish man like Paul, a Hebrew of the Hebrews, to turn the Gentile world upside down for Yeshua.

## LACK OF PASSION AND FAITH-FATIGUE

A lack of passion can hinder vision. Vince Lombardi, coach of the Green Bay Packers football team, put it this way, "Exhaustion makes cowards of us all." It is true. A lack of passion, exhaustion, fatigue can undermine our ability to press to the mark of the higher calling. Look to Him for strength and to be re-energized by the Holy Spirit. It is important for the planter to take care of himself, take time for prayer, personal Shabbat, to be renewed and refreshed in the Lord. Do not let fatigue rob you of your passion and erode your vision.

## SHORT-TERM THINKING

Another more subtle hindrance to vision is short-term thinking. Although we should care for one another, and carry each other's burdens, the planter needs to be careful of short-term thinking and learn to delegate. We often react to people's requests for immediate needs. The planter may be very sweet to oblige, however he might miss the more strategic aspects of the work of the congregation. Therefore, some things require delegation.

## UNQUALIFIED LEADERSHIP

Unqualified leadership is another hindrance to vision. Unqualified planters will need to be involved with more mature leaders, mentored by them so they can understand and share in a unifying vision. Lack of qualified leadership will limit congregational growth.

## TRADITION

Jewish tradition is of great value. Messianic congregations should utilize tradition to communicate the truth. All tradition, which is utilized in service and life, should reflect the truth of Scripture. However, tradition should never replace the truth of Scripture. We need to be aware of the possibility of being diffused in our focus by minor traditional differences. Let us not major in the minors. Yeshua is the vision and the center of everything we do, including fulfillment of the Jewish Scriptures (John 5:39). The vision is in fact all about Yeshua, who is the Head. As His congregation we are the Body of Messiah and, as such, the Body lives out the values of the Head.

If we become distracted from the centrality of Messiah, even by good ideas, it will prove to be disastrous and keep us from serving the Lord. However, as we look unto Yeshua and remain faithful to His vision, we will bring Him glory and honor.

Chapter 3

# Establishing Unifying Values

When the Lord brought us to serve in Charlotte, North Carolina, we actively engaged in evangelism and as a result, many came to faith through our monthly outreaches. We averaged several hundred visitors to our meetings and we began to pray about planting a local congregation. However as we began to form a core group and work on establishing unifying values we found the numbers were reduced to about 10 families. This core group spent the next nine months meeting together, where we worked out not only a unifying vision, but also unifying values in the form of a constitution, our common values list, etc. We understood it would take a risk to form unifying values, yet we knew in the long run there would be stability and healthy growth.

What are unifying values? Values are beliefs put into action. They are principles which serve as guides. This works in the same way as a unifying vision, since a core group requires values to be able to function well together to achieve its goals. It is not enough for a group to share in a set of mere concepts or ideas. There is a need for clear values, which all agree upon and share. In contrast, a lack of unifying values might hinder the work of God.

## UNITY IN WHAT WE BELIEVE

Can two walk together, unless they are agreed? (Amos 3:3)

Thus it is important for a group to clarify its values together. The values, which a planter will set for the group need to be objective and agreed upon by all. Here are five areas of values to consider as you establish values to unify a congregation: 1) Unity regarding beliefs; 2) Unity of goals and direction; 3) Agreement on spiritual gifts; 4) Recognized standards of stewardship; 5) Submission to Yeshua. These areas of values need to be thought through by the planter and presented to the core group for discussion and approval.

### UNITY REGARDING BELIEFS

A congregation needs to have a clear-cut set of articles which identifies the beliefs of the group. Our faith is based on Scripture. "All Scripture is inspired by God and profitable for teaching, for reproof, for correction, for training in righteousness; so that the man of God may be adequate, equipped for every good work" (2 Timothy 3:16-17).

There are primary issues and secondary issues. The secondary issues are those that believers generally may differ on. People of your congregation need to understand the difference between primary and secondary matters. It has been said this way: "Our unity is in the primary teachings. Our liberty is in the secondary teachings. And, we have charity in all things." This means your congregation has to know what is primary and what is secondary. Otherwise they will be arguing about secondary issues all the time, where they should be ready to give liberty.

What are some secondary issues? The Scripture makes it clear in Matthew 23:23. It says Yeshua said they were taxing cumin and other kinds of herbs but forgetting about the weightier issues of justice and mercy. There are weightier issues, primary issues. The secondary issues might deal with attire or food. Other such elements, for example, translation of Scripture and those kinds of things that you will want to distinguish so that people can understand what is important for your congregation. Articles of Faith are to clearly communicate a congregation's primary beliefs.

Therefore, as unifying values are developed they must reflect the will of God. Unifying values will impact our behavior and congregational activities and will serve as the key to congregational unity. One congregation I visited for on-site congregation planting training had a problem in conducting their services. They held a full traditional morning service (*shacharit*), which took an hour and a half, then there was nearly an hour of contemporary praise and worship, and lastly the teaching was given. It might appear this service would meet all the needs of the congregants, but the problem the leadership faced was a large number of attendees were skipping the Torah Service altogether and just showing up for the musical part of worship. As we explored this issue together, we discovered that the leadership was not unified in their values. Some of the leadership valued the liturgy and readings while others did not. Why? They failed to communicate the importance of the traditional service to a large part of the congregation, which would have resulted in greater unity. In this case, the issue was not a matter of the length of the service, but rather a lack of unifying values. Once leadership could see the problem, they purposed to resolve it.

To summarize: The unifying values are not only going to be the Articles of Faith, but also the understanding of what faithfulness means, what is involved with congregational governance, and how things get done. The core group needs to understand the planter's philosophy of ministry so they can faithfully assist and contribute.

## UNITY ABOUT THE MOSAIC LAW

The planter needs to have an established position as to where he stands when it comes to the relationship of the follower of Messiah and the Mosaic Law, and clearly communicate his position to the core group. Each congregation may have its own theoretical twist or *halakhic* nuance in how this matter is defined.

NOTES:

## UNITY ABOUT EVANGELISM

All of us are called to reach the lost and share the Good News. Therefore, the core group needs to share the value of Yeshua's Great Commission (Matthew 28:19). Not all will have the same gifts or strengths, but everyone is in some way involved when it concerns reaching out. If there is no unity in evangelism, the testimony of the congregation will suffer as it becomes ingrown.

## UNITY ABOUT DISCIPLESHIP

There has to be a unity of values regarding the discipleship program. A variety of people may join your congregation; however not all went through good Messianic discipleship. Some might even bring extra baggage of unhealthy teaching. However, it is a responsibility of the planter to evaluate carefully how to implement the program of discipleship based on the community needs, which will result in a wholesome congregation. The undiscipled believer is a dysfunctional member.

## UNITY ABOUT GENTILE BELIEVERS

Another significant area of unifying values is the understanding of Gentile believers and how they fit in the congregational life and ministry. Scripture teaches the Body of Messiah is to be made up of Jew and Gentile together. Although it seems to be a rather simple issue, nonetheless this needs to be discussed and agreed upon.

## UNITY OF GOALS AND DIRECTION

Once I helped to plant a congregation in Connecticut. The man who invited me to assist had been leading Bible studies and Jewish outreach in the area for many years. When we initiated a work of planting a Messianic congregation, he faced an issue of divided commitment. As a long-standing member at a local church, he did not, at first, understand the goal of planting a congregation implied he could not remain an active member of his church, and continue on with assisting in the work of this new plant. Eventually during formation of the core group, he realized the goals of a congregation were different than his outreach fellowship. And, his commitment would involve being a regular in service, tithing, and all other aspects to help a congregation to thrive. Dual membership is a divided commitment.

Therefore, the goals and direction of the congregation needs to be presented and carefully explained by the planter and then accepted by the core group members. When a congregation's goals and direction are understood it will reflect in the level of dedication and commitment to the work.

## AGREEMENT ON SPIRITUAL GIFTS

There has to be a unity on the matter of spiritual gifts, which are given by the Holy Spirit for the purpose of building up of the Body and testimony in the community.

> As each one has received a special gift, employ it in serving one another as good stewards of the manifold grace of God. Whoever speaks, is to do so as one who is speaking the utterances of God; whoever serves is to do so as one who is serving by the strength which God supplies; so that in all things God may be glorified through Yeshua the Messiah, to whom belongs the glory and dominion forever and ever. Amen. (1 Peter 4:10-11).

Therefore, the planter has to make sure that individuals are developing and employing their gifts in order to further the work of God and advancement of the Good News.

NOTES:

All believers are gifted to serve in some capacity, some thirty-fold, some sixty-fold, and some hundred-fold. In the New Covenant we see different lists of gifts for each community (Romans 12; 1 Corinthians 12; Ephesians 4).

## RECOGNIZED STANDARDS OF STEWARDSHIP

In the garment industry, it has been said, "measure twice, cut once." The same principle could be applied to the planning approach of the use of our time, talent and treasure and all that we bring with us in service to the Lord (2 Corinthians 8:16-24).

***Time:*** When it comes to being good stewards of time, Paul exhorts us in Ephesians 5:15-16, "See then that you walk circumspectly, not as fools but as wise, redeeming the time, because the days are evil." As leaders of a congregation we need to lead by example, to start things on time and treasure the time that others voluntarily give.

***Talent:*** In the same way, we are to utilize people's talents in a wise manner. It is easy to take advantage of willing individuals. In order to avoid burn out of individuals who serve diligently, there has to be a plan in place for rotations, encouragement, and appreciation. Furthermore, ensure those who serve are also ministered to and are thriving in their spiritual walk. Perhaps the way to guard them from burn out is "tithing" the amount of time they volunteer for service in the congregation. Giving two to four hours per week would be sufficient for a volunteer group of people. This will keep volunteers healthy and resilient as well. We must avoid burning out willing people.

NOTES:

***Treasure:*** We need to be careful in how we use funds (2 Corinthians 8:20). In the work of God we need to make certain there is no taint on the testimony of Messiah. Sadly, in some congregations this precaution is overlooked. I would suggest the leadership have trustees who will be dedicated to oversee the congregational finances, in order to allow the congregational planter to minister to people. We need to be good stewards of congregational finances and avoid any improper or sloppy control over money.

If people are thinking of joining your congregation plant, they may want to ask to see your budget, and how you plan to utilize the funds. This is a reasonable request. A budget is just a schedule; it is like scheduling your time. It is essential that you schedule how to use your funds in order to accomplish strategic goals for the congregation. Thus, unity of values is seen as proper use of time, talent, and treasure.

## SUBMISSION TO YESHUA

The most important value for unity is submission to the sovereignty of the Lord. Are you and your core group dominated by Yeshua's Lordship? (Philippians 1:21; 1 Corinthians 11:1) Otherwise, the blind will be leading the blind and they may all fall into a ditch. No one wants to be the congregational leader of B'nai Ditch.

It is critical to understand the importance of Yeshua: He being exalted, lifted up and magnified. This is the key issue for a Messianic community. He is the key issue for our testimony and what our lives are all about.

In applying these unifying values, here are things a leader will have to do with a core group:

- Test the assumptions by asking questions. Find out what people actually believe, and where they are.
- Be ready to make disciples. Teach them the wholesome values, which will reflect the congregation.
- Be ready to explain the differences between primary and secondary issues.

Though we have charity in all things, our unity is in the primary issues of our faith. We have liberty in the secondary issues of our faith, and also use secondary issues to express the primary issues. If people do not know the difference between primary and secondary, they will quarrel and divide over anything. Make sure you are clarifying these matters in regard to developing the core group. May the Lord be pleased as we unify around the values, which reflect His character.

Chapter 4

# DEVELOPING A CORE GROUP

Do not lay hands on no one quickly and thereby share responsibility for the sins of others; keep yourself free from sin. (1 Timothy 5:22)

The Scriptures warn us to "lay hands on no one quickly," yet in some cases congregations are planted in haste and may not take adequate time for proper core group development. An example of a baby forming in the womb can help us understand this process. Just as a pre-mature birth of a baby can bring difficulties; likewise, the core group of a congregation needs time to form properly, even before its first congregational service. The process can take anywhere from 5 to 24 months, depending on the group with which you are working. There are three stages to this process:

1. ***The instruction stage***, where the vision and values of the congregation are taught by the planter and embraced by the core group (2 to 12 months);

2. ***The integration stage***, where the various responsibilities and systems of a congregation are covered in detail (2 weeks to 5 months);

3. ***The application stage***, where responsibilities and roles are assessed and assigned to members of the planters' team (3 to 6 months).

(The stages will be also covered in Part III.)

# TEAM ROLES

The core group is made up of both *partners* and *participants*. The planter's wife should be considered a partner in ministry. The planter's spouse could be involved in a variety of different ministries depending on her gifts and abilities (teaching, music, nursery, Shabbat school, and administration); on the other hand, she may have responsibilities of family or work which preclude heavy involvement. Whatever it may be, it is the couple-power that matters. Regardless of her level of involvement, it is important for a planter to value and cherish his spouse as a partner in service, however she is gifted.

The difference between partners and participants will be seen in their level of ownership of the vision and in their capacity to multiply that vision in others. The partners believe God has called them to be involved in this vital task of ministry. Because of their level of commitment, the planter will comfortably share with the partners his concerns as well as the vision and values of the congregation to be planted. The planter can count on the partners to support him though the victories and problems of planting a congregation. Their commitment is to be appreciated and the sacrifices they make are given as a gift to the Lord. Ministry partners may actually be involved in the planting of the congregation in the core group development. They are infectious in their desire for the congregation to be planted as they reach out to others, and are change agents when interacting with others, regarding the values and vision.

Though ideally everyone in the core group could be a partner, in reality many will be committed at a participant level. Over the period of core-group development, the planter will confirm the partners in their roles and expectations.

The majority of members in the core group will be participants. They may be willing to serve in some capacity, though they may not be available at all times. In contrast, the partners may actually stay up at night as much as the planter would, doing all they can to make sure the work of God moves forward. The core-group participants need to have the following characteristics:

1. ***Capable:*** The planter will recognize in the participants skills, experience, and abilities which they will use to further the work, including: teachers, musicians, accountants, and other important tasks vital to the congregation (greeting, setting up chairs, etc.).
2. ***Available:*** They will be available to give of their time and talents to assist in this work. Though a cliché, it is still true that the greatest ability is availability. When there is a need, they can step up and make themselves available for service.

3. ***Responsible:*** They can be trusted in their tasks. Novelty wears off in any service in a congregation, but a planter should look for people with follow-through to complete their service (1 Corinthians 4:2). This is what we look for at every level of responsibility.

4. ***Responsive:*** The planter and his partners may be sharing in the vision of what needs to get done, but the members need to be responsive and manageable in carrying out the work. They have to be able to flex with the leadership when things do not work out and adjust to new plans.

5. ***Enthusiastic:*** They need to have the right attitude before the Lord. They need to know how to "cast their cares on the Lord" (1 Peter 5:7).

6. ***Teachable:*** As followers of Messiah, participants should be willing to learn new skills in service. They may have previously been members and served elsewhere, yet they need to be willing to learn new things. Core group development is meant to get everyone on the same page regarding the distinctions as well as the similarities which the congregation may have in the vision and the values. They have to be teachable in this regard, as they move ahead together in the work of God.

NOTES:

The partners should have all these qualities as well, but would differ on their level of ownership on the vision and values of the congregation. The planter eventually needs to see a clear distinction between partners and participants; otherwise it can lead to disappointment. Partners may not feel appreciated at all when their commitment and ownership is not valued. And it may be too much to expect participants to have the highest level of commitment to the work.

The planter's and partners' responsibilities during core-group development may smoothly transition to elders in the congregation once the congregation is established. Until then, the partners can be seen as elders-in-training in the areas of Prayer, the Word, and Overseer (administration). These three responsibilities will be covered in Part 2.

Various individuals in the core group will fill roles which are essential to the functioning of the congregation.

## RECRUITER/EVANGELIST

Recruiters and evangelists are usually people who have magnetic personalities. They are the networkers, people who can reach out in the community with others, eventually inviting people to meetings and services. These individuals are quite involved and can motivate others in their involvement.

## TEACHERS

Teaching will need to be carried out at various levels (including different ages and genders), and it is not preferable for the planter to be the only teacher. People who can teach biblical truth in various settings will be needed. All teachers need to agree fully with the vision and values of the congregation.

## CHILDREN'S MINISTRY LEADER

It is extremely important to have someone who can faithfully minister to children. A congregation is a community of families joined together and the children are the future of the congregation if we do not want merely a one generation congregation. We want to see all the children become disciples of Messiah, and this is not an automatic process. A leader for children's ministry should love kids, but more importantly is able to plan, lead, recruit, and train others in the ministry to children.

## PRAYER/WORSHIP LEADER

We need someone able to plan, recruit, and train others in worship and prayer. This is of vital importance, and will also have to fit into the needs for format and style of prayer and worship, whether it is more liturgical or informal. You will want to find people who will be able to lead in worship, praise and in prayer. This role may eventually become the ministry of a cantor or worship leader in the congregation. Once more, all people involved in the worship ministry should certainly agree on the congregation's vision and values before being placed up front.

## SHEPHERD/CARE GIVERS

This role is for someone who is relational, intentionally caring for the people around them. A shepherd reaches out to those that may be in need, hurting, or wounded. A congregation must care for the weakest, as Messiah prioritizes. Thus the planter will have to have other people on the team who will be reaching out and caring for the least among us.

## FINANCIAL/BUSINESS ADMINISTRATOR

Another role is someone who could handle funds, a financial or business administrator. This person must be trust-worthy. This individual might eventually be asked to assist in designing systems of accountability in the congregation (as a non-profit, etc.). These positions must be filled by people of impeccable integrity.

NOTES:

## ORGANIZER/IMPLEMENTER

Another area of need is to have someone who can organize and put together various teams. Oneg, greeters, and other areas of ministry tend to require rotating teams and so this role would need strong administrative and people skills.

All these roles are a part of a core-group team development. The process by which these matters will be implemented will be covered in Part 3.

# PART 2

# PLANTING MESSIANIC CONGREGATIONS

## Chapter 5

# CONGREGATION PLANTING ROOTED IN YESHUA'S WORK

In this part, we will delve into the responsibilities and systems of a Messianic congregation. Opinions vary as to what a Messianic congregation is and what form it should take. I understand a congregation to be a community of Messianic disciples in loving accountability to one another. From Jethro's counsel to Moses in Exodus 18:19-22 (as it is aslo applied in Acts 6:1-7; 1 Timothy 2:8-15), there are three responsibilities that help produce this loving accountability. These responsibilities are:

1. ***Prayer***
2. ***Ministry of the Word***
3. ***Overseer*** (Figure 2.0)

*Figure 2.0*

As disciples of the Messiah, such communities are called to live out three essential responsibilities, which are rooted in the work of Messiah Himself. The functionality of a Messianic congregation is seen through the Body expressing the redemptive priorities of the Head through the exercise of these responsibilities. The Body of Messiah is to be praying, ministering the Word, overseeing and administering the work of God.

Moreover, these three responsibilities: Prayer, ministry of the Word, and overseer, are rooted in the person of Messiah Himself, in light of His own three-fold work as Priest, Prophet, and King. Messiah is our High Priest according to the order of Melchizedek (Psalm 110:4). He is the prophet "like Moses"—not only did He prophetically minister the Word, but He is the Living Word (Deuteronomy 18:15-19). Finally, He is the King of kings, the greater son of David (Isaiah 9:6-7). He oversees our activities by His absolute authority, reigning over our hearts and lives. His ministry is what we are to live out in our spheres of influence—in our hearts, homes, and congregations.

When some think about what a Messianic congregation is, they may have in mind a particular model of worship services, or meeting on Saturday instead of Sunday. In fact, worship models and styles will vary depending on the leader's convictions and the environment. A group may find that they need to shift to a more appropriate model, or adopt a multifaceted approach. Therefore, let us consider several varieties within the Messianic movement.

***A traditional religious model*** would follow a traditional, normative Jewish format. The Shabbat services may follow the pattern of opening traditional prayers, the *Shema* and its blessings, the *Amidah,* climaxing with a Torah service, the message and then closing prayer. Many Messianic congregations reflect this traditional order in their own services. Depending on the congregation, the particular model may run the gamut of the religious expression in the Jewish world, from Orthodox tradition (no instrumental music, separation of sexes) to Reform (tallit optional, use of instruments in worship).

***In a contemporary Messianic model,*** Shabbat services will contain some of the traditional liturgy (the *Shema* and *Birkat HaKohanim*, for example) and mixed with contemporary Messianic worship music, which arose in the last few generations. Within the service, emphasis is placed on the message from the Scriptures. This model is often effective in speaking to communities where the majority of Jewish people are not religiously oriented.

***A Messianic Sunday model*** might seem a bit unusual, however there are some large and well-known congregations with this approach. The services will emphasize sensitivity in communicating the Good News with a Messianic orientation in the language and songs. They may have Friday Bible studies as well as Sunday morning services. They will likely observe the Jewish Festivals.

NOTES:

What factors into determining the style? One factor is the planter's own personal conviction. For example, if a planter believes that God wants the Jewish people to maintain traditions in their worship, then this conviction will determine the model of the congregation. If one considers one particular model to be legitimate or authentic Messianic faith and others inauthentic, then he will be restrained by those convictions, and understandably so. Consequently, the planter may also be restricted by the community he is in. This is reflected in Paul's methodology:

> For though I am free from all men, I have made myself a slave to all, so that I may win more. To the Jews I became as a Jew, so that I might win Jews; to those who are under Torah, as under Torah though not being myself under Torah, so that I might win those who are under Torah; to those who are without Torah, as without Torah, though not being without the Torah of God but under the Torah of Messiah, so that I might win those who are without Torah. (1 Corinthians 9:19-21).

Paul's flexible *halakhah* for the sake of the Good News may have led to various models of service which differed between observant and secularized communities. However, a Messianic congregation must have a calling, which goes deeper than its style.

"As He (Messiah) is, so are we in the world" (1 John 4:17). Yeshua is the Head, and we are the Body (Ephesians 4:15-16). The body lives out the values of the head. Messianic congregations are called not to a particular style of service, but to the work of Messiah Himself.

Therefore, we will consider the responsibility of prayer and worship as it reflects Yeshua who "always lives to make intercession for us" (Hebrews 7:25). As He intercedes for us, so also the ministry of the congregation must be led and undergirded by prayer.

We will consider the systems and role of teaching which are found in the ministry of the Word, which testifies of Him who is the Truth. Indeed, "the testimony of Yeshua is the Spirit of prophecy" (Revelation 19:10). The ministry of the Messianic congregation is the Word both living and written.

Finally, as we consider the responsibility of overseer (and administration), we will learn how the other ministries are determined to be carried out decently and in order. This reflects King Messiah, who orders and reigns in all things.

The end result is to make the name of Yeshua known in all the earth. His values, character, and name are to be honored and exalted in the life of His body.

NOTES:

## Chapter 6

# PRAYER AND WORSHIP

I think of prayer as the most important responsibility for a congregation. In fact, this may be the only aspect of congregational life taking place in *olam haba* (the world to come). In light of this, the ministry of prayer is preparing us for our future home.

Prayer and worship can be considered together because, whether it is in singing or speaking, both prayer and worship are praises and supplications directed to the Lord and intended to bless and bring honor to Him. The worship itself could be in an instrumental arrangement or a cappella, even so it is all to be praise and prayer unto HaShem.

Biblical teaching must be at the heart of prayer and worship ministry. The Samaritans did not have sound teaching, and thus it was wrong even if it was sincere (John 4:22-23). Worship has the additional by-product of further discipling *talmidim* in the truth. From a communications perspective, there are three means of carrying truth directly to the heart: humor, pathos, and music. People will often think about what they sang in worship. The worship may bring the truth of God and His salvation deeper into their souls. Therefore, sound teaching must be the basis of our prayer and worship.

Worship teams need to be prayer leaders, that is, men and women with a strong prayer life. A good voice and musical skills have value, but are no substitute for prayer. An individual's prayer and worship life helps foster his or her healthy relationship with the Lord, and so all team members must desire deeper levels of prayer and worship. It is a matter both of personal growth and integrity before the Lord.

## AN ELDER-LED RESPONSIBILITY

HaShem teaches that His house "would be a house of prayer" (Isaiah 56:7). This primacy of prayer is further seen in the history of our people.

### IN THE TORAH

In Exodus 17, the first battle after Israel came out of Egypt was with the Amalekites. In this portion of Scripture we find there was a division of labor. Joshua took the army and fought the Amalekites while Moses, along with Aaron and Hur went to the top of the mountain and with arms outstretched to God, we find them praying. That prayer ministry was the key issue in the victory. Moses' arms coming down pictured the stopping of prayer, that is, stopping our dependence on God and our abiding in Yeshua. At those times, the army of Joshua failed. Prayer was and is the essential issue in victory—for Israel, for our homes, and for our congregations. It prepared us as a people, as to how we were to live in the land. Future victories would result from prayer.

In Exodus 17:14 Moses says, "Write this down for Joshua to read." Why is Joshua singled out? Perhaps as an action-oriented man and leader of soldiers, he would need to be reminded to pray since his natural response might be to merely fight in his own strength. When we read the book of Joshua, we see that Joshua only had two defeats. In Joshua 7, he prayed only after the defeat; and in Joshua 9, he did not pray before negotiating with an enemy. His two defeats resulted directly from a lack of prayer. A lack of prayer can also be the cause for defeat for any congregation which gets established, consequently victory comes as leaders lead in prayer.

### IN THE NEW COVENANT

Paul tells Timothy that in the congregation there is to be prayer "first of all" (1 Timothy 2:1). Our community life is to be a *beit teflilah,* house of prayer. Benedictions, supplications, intercession, praise—all types of prayer ministries are part of our prayer priority. However, elder-led prayer is biblically normative. Men everywhere were to lift holy hands in worship, and so men are normally to be leading in prayer (1 Timothy 2:8). Why would they have to be instructed to do that? Perhaps to show that prayer would be primary in how a man manages his own home (1 Timothy 3:5). If men are not leading in prayer at home, how can we expect them to lead in prayer in the congregation?

Not only do we want to make sure we are praying as a community, we want the leaders to be praying for the community. Who knows what battles our "Joshuas" are fighting at home, school and at work? In fact, one of the marks of spiritual leadership is that they lead in prayer. In the Biblical picture of heaven, the elders are forever falling down on their face before God, leading in prayer. They are prayer and worship leaders. Whether in the home or in the congregation, prayer prepares us for heavenly service like nothing else.

## HEARTS FOR THE LORD

People need to be taught to pray. It should be part of basic *talmidut* (discipleship), and should not be assumed, especially with transfer growth. Many men, who I have discipled long after they came to personal faith in Yeshua, confided in me they did not have a fervent prayer life, and did not feel comfortable praying out loud. These men were able to slide through, by just showing up, without any spiritual ministry expected of them. The Messianic congregation is the place for people to grow as praying disciples.

### LITURGY AND INTENTIONALITY

All prayer should be from the heart. In this regard, there is no distinction between formal liturgical prayers, which the congregation prays, and more informal prayers.

NOTES:

There is certainly a value to Hebrew being used for continuity with the greater Jewish community, but a problem arises when the prayers (or worship songs) are in Hebrew, and the congregation does not understand the language. Praying with intention (*kavanah*) and understanding is supposed to be a value in traditional Judaism as well. Nevertheless, many will use the liturgy by rote without regard to how well the words are personally understood. From the opposite end, it is just as problematic when some evangelical worship services are evaluated by how much of a "worship experience" it is to those participating. We worship to honor HaShem, not merely to get something out of prayer service. One of the ways we must evaluate the service is by how well it is understood. As Paul wrote to the Corinthians:

> Therefore let one who speaks in a tongue pray that he may interpret. If I pray in a tongue, my spirit prays, but my mind is unfruitful. What is the outcome then? I will pray with the spirit and I will pray with the mind also; I will sing with the spirit and I will sing with the mind also. Otherwise if you bless in the spirit only, how will the one who fills the place of the ungifted say the "Amen" at your giving of thanks, since he does not know what you are saying? For you are giving thanks well enough, but the other person is not edified. (1 Corinthians 14:13-17)

All public prayer and worship songs should be understood in the language of the community, conducted not only with sincerity of heart, but for the edification of others.

Community must have an understanding also regarding how their prayer is *b'Shem Yeshua* (in the name of Yeshua). Of course, I am not saying a formula "*b'Shem Yeshua*" should be added to the end of every prayer. Rather, the prayer and worship must be conducted in His name, to the honor of His name. Where Yeshua is not honored, as a follower of the Messiah, it would not be true worship. All Messianic synagogues are to be oriented in their prayer and worship toward Yeshua, since as our Intercessor (Hebrews 7:25). He taught us that "no one comes to the Father but by Him" (John 14:6). This is the expectation of the *Shlichim* (Apostles) as well:

> Speaking to one another in psalms and hymns and spiritual songs, singing and making melody with your heart to the Lord; always give thanks for everything to God the Father in the name of our Lord Yeshua the Messiah. (Ephesians 5:19-20)

As a congregational value on prayer, it makes sense to teach people to pray in Hebrew. However, at the very least, there would need to be translation for visitors to the congregation (1 Corinthians 14:16). Moreover, one has to be careful of a divided membership (between the elite who can do the prayers and those who cannot). These matters need to be carefully worked out to the edification of all, and will be handled differently according to the differences of various communities.

NOTES:

## ORDER AND EDIFICATION

Certain demonstrative activities (tongues and prophecy in worship) are management matters, and not necessarily doctrinal in nature. Since "everything is to be done decently and in order," if someone has a word to be shared with the congregation, it can be given to the leadership, who can evaluate to see whether it would be edifying for the whole congregation, or is better kept private (1 Corinthians 14:40). In general, I would suggest that what is said in the prayer closet is for one's own edification; whereas, what is said in the congregation must be for everyone's edification (Figure 2.1).

| Private Prayer | Public Prayer |
|---|---|
| Understandable to God (Romans 8:26) | Understandable to others (1 Corinthians 14:16-17) |
| As long as you want (Luke 6:12) | Succinct (Matthew 6:7-8) |
| Always and Constantly (1 Thessalonians 5:17) | Prioritized and Regular (1 Timothy 2:1) |
| Freely and openly (1 Peter 5:7) | Of sound mind and sensibly (2 Corinthians 5:13) |
| For one's own edification (1 Corinthians 14:2, 28) | For everyone's edification (1 Corinthians 14:16-17) |

*Figure 2.1*

## MUSIC IN WORSHIP

One of the primary things the Messianic community is known for is the great amount of music it has produced, especially from its pioneer generations. When it was first coming out, the music was seen as cutting edge, even as Messianic ministry was seen as doing something new in reaction to the normal Gentile cultural expression of worship in the greater Body of Messiah.

NOTES:

Times change, and that same music with its minor key credentials do not always have the same impact. Our worship as it develops must remain decidedly Messianic, however, every generation and community will have to find its own appropriate expression of worship. I am a proponent of experimentation and communities attempting new forms with the same scriptural values. It is the worship of HaShem that ultimately matters and not the musicians or musical style. In the end, we must seek to make music, which is truly worshipful so people can readily worship.

There are practical matters to consider with regard to length of worship and prayer. We considered in Part 1 how in a congregational services with a full liturgy and Torah service and rather full instrumental worship set, attendees have come for part, for example, the last hour and a half of a three hour service. Families and older congregants can only handle so much. If there is a desire for especially long worship service, it may be right to have special nights set aside for just that. I would suggest the worship leader (if there is one as well as the planter) not be permitted to extend the worship as long as he or she sees fit, but rather the leadership team should discuss these matters in advance. In some worship services, it appears that there will be an award for true worshipper given to the "last man standing." Worship leaders require restraint from wearing out the congregation at least as much as the Bible teachers do (I admit I am still growing in this matter, too).

## DEVELOPING IN PRAYER AND WORSHIP

All services in the beginning will be relative to the personnel and training available. However, even with limited personnel, making priority of a public prayer actually reinforces to the core group the importance of prayer as essential value to the fellowship. Every gathering should begin and end with prayer and considered a norm in the life of the congregation. "Pray always" is an intentional lifestyle choice for the mature believer and the maturing congregation (1 Thessalonians 5:17).

### QUALIFIED LEADERS

There are certain qualifications for those involved in prayer ministry. Those leading a prayer team must be people of prayer. In general, for public prayer, as well as for leading a prayer ministry for the congregation, those who are in front leading prayer should be able to represent the congregation and minister after the service. Visitors may likely to consider whoever is up front must be a leader, who can, therefore, answer questions representing the congregation. The temptation in the beginning stage of the congregation is to let anybody who is willing to step up, but we must remember how visitors will perceive it (1 Timothy 3:8; 5:22). Over time more leaders will be trained and entrusted to represent the values which come with the responsibility.

NOTES:

## CONFIDENTIALITY IN PRAYER

Because of the sensitive nature of prayer needs, one must be a member of the congregation, in my opinion, to receive the prayer requests. Only those who share the values of the synagogue can share in the problems and their solutions through prayer. A prayer team must value discretion, keeping all prayer needs sent to them confidentially. One must not talk to any others, even a spouse, about what one learns in prayer about another member's personal issues. If these prayer needs are publicized in some way (in email, etc.), care must be taken that they must not be passed along outside the congregation. It may seem obvious, but people need to be informed as a policy, and this policy needs to be enforced. I have had the unenviable task of removing gossips from the prayer ministry. Also problems arise when spouses use public prayer for their 'beloved', which would only embarrass the person being prayed for.

Therefore prayer requests for a third party should not be voiced within the congregation if that person has not requested public prayer.

Prayer and worship is the priority for a Messianic congregation. It undergirds the Ministry of the Word by bringing us into communion with God through Yeshua our High Priest and Intercessor. As such, it should be God-honoring, Yeshua-oriented, edifying to all, understandable, not overlong, and Biblically sound in content.

## Chapter 7

# MINISTRY OF THE WORD

The ministry of the Word has two dimensions of service: inward and outward. Within the body of Messiah, the Word (Torah) provides edification, and outside the body, that same Word ministers evangelization. The Word testifies of Yeshua, and "the testimony of Yeshua is the spirit of prophecy" (Revelation 19:10). We proclaim the Living Word according to the written Word, and proclaim the written Word to exalt the Living Word.

The two-dimensional ministry of the Word can further be understood by considering four interlocking systems: contact-making, disciple-making, member-making, and leader-making. *(See figure 2.2)*

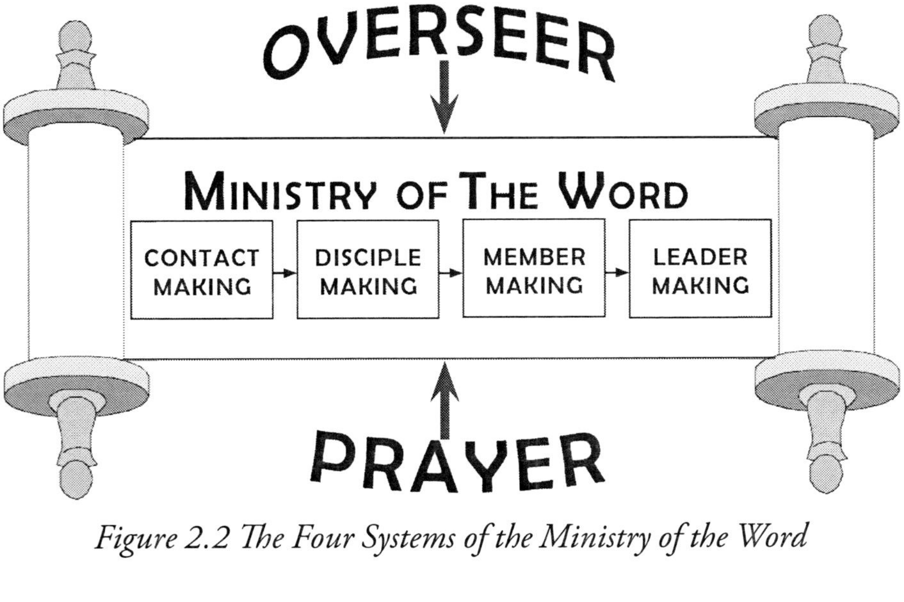


*Figure 2.2 The Four Systems of the Ministry of the Word*

We will consider these four systems and then consider the application in teaching the Word (Ecclesiastes 12:9-12).

## THE CONTACT-MAKING SYSTEM

The ministry of the Word, as it deals with evangelization, is called contact making. The reason it is called "contact-making" is because the effectiveness of this system is evaluated and developed on whether or not we end up with contacts.

## THE CALL TO REACH OUT

Reaching out with one's faith is a normal practice of all followers of Messiah. The Scriptures teach that the redeemed will share their faith with others (Psalm 107:2). All believers are enabled by the Holy Spirit to share their faith:

> But you will receive power when the Holy Spirit has come upon you, and you will be my witnesses in Jerusalem, in all Judea and Samaria, and even to the ends of the earth. (Acts 1:8)

Ultimately, only the Father through the Spirit draws people to Yeshua (John 6:44). However, our faithfulness is found in how we handle our stewardship. In this case our stewardship as we reach out is to be making contacts. It may be a name, an e-mail address, or something which allows us to follow-up with that person. All congregations are called to proclaim the Good News of Messiah "to the Jew first and also to the Gentile" (Romans 1:16). This system of contact making needs to be developed within the congregation, and reaching out should be a part of a congregation's DNA.

NOTES:

### VISION AND VALUES

The goal of contact making is to see people "know Messiah and make Him known" (Colossians 1:27), that is, for individuals to come to personal faith in Messiah Yeshua, and then enter into Messianic discipleship where they become grounded and rooted in the faith, and as His followers will then effectively share Messiah with others. The values of contact making especially emphasize:

- ***Confidence*** - We are "not ashamed of the Good News."
- ***Integrity*** - We will do nothing misleading to neither tarnish His name nor withhold the only means of salvation.
- ***Love*** - Messiah's love constrains our hearts to proclaim the only message, which can save lost people, Jewish people and Gentiles alike.

## CONTACT MAKING PROCESS

This system is made up of a three-step process:

1. ***Find them***
2. ***File them***
3. ***Follow them up.***

***First of all, find them.*** There should be all kinds of outreach in the community, whether through a website, social media, newspaper ads, or meeting people through street evangelism. It is not about any specific tactic or method, rather the point is to find people. There are many ways this happens through a congregation:

- ✡ *Community activities:* these activities are an outworking of our commitment to demonstrate that Yeshua is God's faithfulness to Israel and the nations. These activities will include prayer (Psalm 122:6; Romans 10:1), public support for Israel and the greater Jewish community in general, and involvement in activities in the greater community.
- ✡ *Profiled activities:* these include holiday services, concerts and other outreaches, that is, meetings where those outside the faith are especially invited, as well as public communication regarding the Good News in general.
- ✡ *Public evangelistic activities:* these are activities where individuals and teams will engage in Messianic literature distribution, street preaching; flash mobs; door-to-door outreach, surveys, etc.
- ✡ *Private small group meetings:* these include *havurot*, dinner parties, and Torah studies which relate to reaching out. Generally these are attended by invitation to friends and word-of-mouth to other interested individuals. Though the goal, as far as a congregation is concerned, is still to make contacts for follow-up with the desire for the salvation of those who do not yet believe, the believers involved need to be especially sensitive to the dynamic of a small group meeting, which is more informal and much more relational.
- ✡ *Personal evangelistic activity:* discipled Messianic believers are to be sharing their faith as a regular part of their lifestyles and relationships. The believers involved in these activities could even get training to assist them in having spiritual discussions with friends and neighbors, which may include Messianic apologetics, addressing frequently asked

NOTES:

questions, and even training on how to teach the Bible, and so on. In every situation all believers are encouraged to reach all individuals who HaShem places in their path.

A congregation will also want to make contact with those who are visiting the congregation, communicating friendliness to help make visitors feel welcomed. I think of greeters as the first line of evangelism inside a congregational building. Greeters also serve to help the visitors feel welcomed by giving them a bulletin and showing them where to go for classes or where to sit in a large service. Greeters are not really for the regulars, who likely know their way around and what they are doing at the service. Greeters are the first witnesses of a congregation so they would need to be people who can represent the congregation to the visitors, with a friendly demeanor as they allow the love of Messiah to control their hearts. In this regard, the greeters should model the values of contact making.

***First, a congregation handles reaching out and finding contacts*** in light of their own environment and culture. Trusting the Lord, we find people who are being sought by Messiah Himself.

***Second, there needs to be a means to file their information.*** Contact information should be put into a database so there is a way to protect it and make it accessible to the people entrusted to use it. This is evidently an administrative function, so people can be part of the general contact making team though they may not have gifts that one might normally associate with evangelism.

NOTES:

***Third, follow them up.*** A team needs to be ready to use the information to reach out to people and minister to them. In many cases, the contact made may be more general in nature and allow for a more general follow-up: thanking them for visiting the service, letting them know of other congregational activities in their area, and inviting them back to the service again. Other times, there will be opportunity to share Messiah and lead them to the Lord, or they may have come to faith but need to be discipled and encouraged in the things of God.

## THE DISCIPLE-MAKING SYSTEM

Inevitably, contact making naturally flows into the need to make disciples. It is not appropriate for a group to focus on "birthing children" without any intention of raising them. The congregation is a place for discipleship. We make contacts to make disciples.

In fact, discipleship is the primary purpose of a congregation. People are not only to be believers, but also followers of the Lord and who know their identity in Messiah; who pray, know the Scriptures, value fellowship, and share their faith; who understand and articulate primary truths of the faith; and who are immersed participants in the community. This process is life long and grounded believers continue to grow into the fullness of the stature of the Messiah (Ephesians 4:13-16; Romans 8:29).

## "20/20 VISION": PUBLICLY AND HOUSE-TO-HOUSE

In disciple-making, the Word is being inculcated and developed at both a larger scale and a smaller scale. According to Acts 20:20, Paul was speaking to those he had discipled, who were now leaders of the congregation at Ephesus. He reminded them of the time spent with them, of his investment into their lives:

> You yourselves know... how I kept back nothing that was profitable, but proclaimed it to you, and taught you publicly and from house to house. (Acts 20:20)

Paul says he "taught you publicly." A Biblically strong *bema* ministry in the congregation is vital, because proper discipleship includes one receiving public teaching. Thus, when individuals want personal teaching (including counseling), I encourage them to come to services regularly (Hebrews 10:25). In this way, they can grasp the big picture from weekly expository messages.

NOTES:

However, Paul also taught "from house to house." He encouraged personal application for the believer from the principles he gave publicly. Paul was not merely being sociable, but was seeking to build up their individual lives and families.

Thus, in addition to public teaching, there needs to be personal discipleship of individuals. Private meetings take the form of both one-on-one and small group meetings. The private ministry is not only instruction, but also application of the Word to individual lives. Personal issues which are inappropriate to be proclaimed from the *bema* still require counsel, encouragement, and even correction for believers of all levels of maturity.

Discipleship may also deal with the basic level of a healthy relationship with the Lord, understanding the sound teaching that reflects our faith in the Messiah and practical application in our homes and community. New believers need to be individually grounded and rooted in the Messianic faith. Growing believers need to learn how to serve the Lord. Those that are maturing need to care for others, if they are indeed maturing in Messiah.

Paul says that in his teaching he "kept back nothing that was profitable," that is, useful and beneficial to their spiritual lives. From this we learn aspects of the content of his discipleship work. The phrase "kept back" in Acts 20:20 was used by the rabbis in the Septuagint (Greek text of the Hebrew Bible) to show partiality, as when Job responds to his friends for their speeches to him: "Will you show partiality for God?" (Job 13:8). In discipleship all need the same instruction, training, encouragement and correction, we must not show partiality to anyone. Even the most difficult subjects of the Scriptures must be dealt with both publicly and privately. Leadership demands holy *chutzpah* and boldness to stand for the truth.

## PREACHING AND TEACHING

Paul states that he both proclaimed to them and taught them. This corresponds to the activities of preaching and teaching as found in 1 Timothy 5:17, "Let the elders who rule well be considered worthy of double honor, especially those who work hard at preaching and teaching." Both are needed to complete and mature the believer.

To "proclaim" is to reveal, announce, or openly divulge the truth (1 John 1:5; Deuteronomy 5:5; Psalm 92:15). This underlies the importance of a strong preaching component at a Saturday service (2 Timothy 4:2), which may be longer and more forceful than the normal *drash* at some non-messianic services.

NOTES:

To "teach" carries a different sense, "to instruct in order to be carried out" (2 Timothy 2:2). We find that the reason for teaching is clearly given in both Hebrew Scriptures and the New Covenant. Note that in Deuteronomy 4:14 Moses says, "The Lord commanded me at that time to teach you statutes and judgments, that you might perform them." And Messiah reiterates the purpose for discipleship in Matthew 28:20 when He says to His disciples, "teaching them to observe (heed or do) all that I commanded you."

***Profitable*** means what is appropriate (Proverbs 19:10). It's not what is merely permitted, but what is good for the believer (1 Corinthians 6:12; 10:23; 12:7). Teachers are not to "tickle the ears" of their listeners with some new spiritual fad (Acts 17:21), but to help each believer grow in the grace of God.

Paul details the teaching further in Acts 20:21, "solemnly testifying to both Jews and Greeks of repentance toward God and faith in our Lord Yeshua the Messiah."

***Testifying*** is used in Luke 16:28 to mean warning. We mentioned that humor, like music and emotion, can be a helpful way to communicate a point; however, the message itself is profoundly serious. Whenever one teaches the Word of

God, one never preaches an unimportant message. The issues are vital and eternal.

***To both Jews and Greeks.*** The unique unity we have in Messiah means no one may be excluded. Messianic leaders are to preach and teach what is sufficient and right for all people, which results in unity in Yeshua. This unique unity is Messiah's unique testimony of Yeshua's fulfillment of God's promise to Abraham, "in you all the families of the earth will be blessed" (Genesis 12:3).

***Repentance and faith.*** This means, turning from sin and trusting in the Lord. The focus is not merely on what we have given up, but to Whom we have turned and entrusted our lives. This encompasses the grace of God and the whole counsel of God.

> Therefore I testify to you this day that I am innocent of the blood of all men. For I have not shunned to declare to you the whole counsel of God. (Acts 20:26-27)

A directive style of expository teaching helps the congregation to understand the focus of the Scriptures. The congregation is the place to give full discipleship, teaching the whole counsel of God.

## THE MEMBER-MAKING SYSTEM

NOTES:

The next system to consider within a congregation is a result of the preceding. We make contacts in order to make disciples; and we make disciples who are functioning members of the Body of Messiah. Though this process lasts a lifetime, we grow as disciples by being functioning members of the Body (Ephesians 4:15-16). Therefore, the result for the congregation is a functioning member in the Body of Messiah. Disciples who commit to congregational values and covenant in order to be serving in that congregation are what we define as members.

### MEMBERSHIP MATTERS

Is membership a good thing, or just another vestige of tradition? Let us consider the roots of this matter. Before there were synagogues, members of the community of Israel were assumed to agree and heed the Torah of Moses, *Brit Milah* (for men), the sacrificial system, and *tevilah*; otherwise they were removed from the people of Israel (Deuteronomy 13:5; 17:12; 21:21; 22:21). In this regard, the town functioned as a sort of congregation. It was at the local level that elders handled benevolence, discipline, blessing, and teaching (Deuteronomy 13:12-18; 14:28-29).

By the time of Yeshua, the synagogue represented the town or community in a sense (John 9:22; 12:42; 16:2; Acts 15:21). Normal precautions would mean that letters of commendation were sent when people would move around from one congregation to another (1 Corinthians 16:3; 2 Corinthians 3:1; 8:18-24). The leaders knew who the believers were, who had publicly declared their faith in Messiah, as it goes on to speak of certain 'unbelievers' entering in (1 Corinthians 14:23-25). Some persons at a gathering were recognized as not part of the actual fellowship.

Today, congregational membership is essential for a healthy congregation. First, congregational discipline for disorder presupposes an admission to fellowship by the acceptance of agreed standards (Matthew 18:15-17; 1 Corinthians 5:13).

Second, a leader should know who he is responsible for in his ministry, in order to properly provide correction, counsel, and encouragement. The elders of a congregation cannot be responsible for the personal growth of every individual who visits the congregation or attends sporadically. Rather, they are primarily responsible to shepherd and instruct those who have submitted to their care and authority. Those they shepherd are also those who serve, representing the congregation to the greater Jewish community and world around them.

Third, Hebrews 13:17 says to those who believe, "Obey your leaders, and submit to them." The question for each believer is, "Who are your leaders?" A believer does not have leaders if he has refused to join a local congregation and submit to the authority of those elders. Thus, such a person cannot obey Hebrews 13:17. For a believer to clearly know to whom he has submitted, assumes clearly defined membership (1 Thessalonians 5:14).

NOTES:

## AGREED VALUES

There are certain goals by which we evaluate and integrate new members into the life of the congregation. Matters discussed earlier—vision, values, and culture—these matters will come to the forefront as people become members.

Classes will be needed to properly teach on what it means to be a member. These classes may reflect the training which is conducted during core group development. Only if the values are taught and discussed will members share these same values. If they come from a different community you should expect that they would have some different values and forms of expression. Therefore, they may actually not fit well into the community if they are not properly taught on why they should value what the congregation values. The classes provide a means to understand what makes this congregation distinct and what they are committing to by joining this particular congregation and not a different one. You may find that some people know the jargon well, but may not understand the values at all. You need to interview each person and evaluate properly so that the unity of the congregation is based on a mutual commitment to the same values.

The values of the congregation not only need to be taught, but also written down so they can be reviewed. Articles of Faith are essential to understand that the primary teachings (doctrines) are the actual unity of faith in the community, and what it means to be followers of Yeshua in this congregation.

## ACTIVE SERVICE

Active members need to be functioning as serving members. The result of discipleship is not merely well-taught people, but empowered servants, not just hearers but doers of the Word. Yeshua put it this way in John 13:17, "If you know these things blessed are you who do them." Implementation of the truth is what Torah (Divine Instruction) is all about. When someone becomes a member of the congregation, that individual is actually committing to active service in that congregation. In this way, the members will be edifying one another for the growth of the congregation in love (Ephesians 4:16).

All of these matters need to be reviewed in classes with whatever training and instruction is needed for people to function well as members.

## STRUCTURE FOR MEMBER-MAKING SYSTEM

NOTES:

The structure for the member making system has several parts.

***Instruction/Orientation Classes.*** These can range anywhere from five to twenty classes. It depends on what instruction is needed. Some people who come to your congregation may not be rooted and grounded in the faith. They may not have a prayer life, do not study the Scriptures, nor follow the Lord, therefore they need to be discipled, in order to become a functioning member of Messiah's Body.

A functioning membership in the congregation requires a discipled membership. Otherwise, if they are not functioning, then they are dysfunctional, and a leader should be wary of incorporating dysfunctional people into the membership. First, they should be grounded and rooted in the faith, so that they may become a healthy part of the community. Remember, the undiscipled believer is a dysfunctional member.

***Interviews.*** Once people have gone through the classes and learn about the values, which make up the community, they should be interviewed so as to make certain that they understand, agree with, and will freely commit to these values. Thus there should be an interview, evaluation, and approval process to become a member of the congregation. This process may also require background checks. Obviously, someone with a criminal record of child molestation should not be involved within the Children's Ministry, and an individual who has been convicted of embezzlement should not be made a trustee. This may only be discovered through a background check. This is not meant to prevent repentant individuals from becoming members. However, it may be unwise to place even repentant individuals in those same positions of responsibility for the sake of the congregation's testimony and security. Also, if they desire to transfer their membership from another congregation (or church), it may be important that they do not have outstanding issues or grievances there. Where there were past quarrels, amends may need to be made for the sake of the whole body of Messiah.

***Integration into Service.*** Integration is a responsibility to involve new members into the various activities in the congregation. During the first year I would advise that new members not be given too much responsibility. They need to show faithfulness in ministry during the first year before being given any leadership role. You may want them involved in small group activities or other service areas within the congregation, to give them various opportunities to develop in their gifts in the Lord. This brings us to our fourth system of the ministry of the Word.

NOTES:

## THE LEADER-MAKING SYSTEM

The congregation develops leaders from the membership, members from those who are growing disciples, and disciples from those who were initially contacts. Our systems should reflect leaders who are properly discipled and are members of the congregation.

Leadership is really an aspect of maturity to which all believers are called. Leadership is not a matter of a strong personality but of a spiritual responsibility. When a mature believer is part of a congregation they will take initiative to care for and serve those around them. Leadership roles come as they effectively care for others. This is actually the spiritual goal for every member of the congregation, and every person that comes to faith in the Messiah.

### LEADERSHIP DEVELOPMENT

A proper approach to leadership development may require a transformation of the way it is understood. First of all, it is the objective of competent discipleship. People become spiritually mature if they are grounded and rooted in the truth.

Leaders are those who grow in the truth of the Word, properly growing in the love of God, and in the grace of God.

There was a man who lost his job after holding it for twenty years. He asked, "How can you fire me after twenty years of service and experience?" The boss responded, "Twenty years? You merely have one year of experience twenty times!" Being a believer for a number of years does not in itself make one mature or ready to be placed into leadership. Thus a vision of growing to maturity is vital. We need people who are being conformed to the image of Messiah.

Secondly, there are obstacles to completing discipleship. To complete discipleship one needs a Spirit-led vision. Only Holy Spirit can give motivation to grow and mature in our spiritual life. Yet, the call is for all people to be Spirit-led. Dealing with the subject of leadership, Paul says that "if any man aspires to the office of overseer, it is a fine work he desires to do"—any man, indeed (1 Timothy 3:1).

It is not being an "alpha male" which makes a leader. It may make someone strong willed and stubborn, but not necessarily a leader. As noted before and it bears repeating, leadership is a responsibility not a personality trait. For example, if you are a parent, then for better or worse, you are a leader. In fact, as soon as you got married, you just became the leader of a new home. A leader is someone who takes and maturely handles his (or her) responsibility. We all have responsibilities as we mature in the Lord.

A Spirit-led vision can lead to a Spirit-led victory. The key is whether one is following the Lord and taking responsibility—first in the heart, then in the home, and finally in the congregation (1 Timothy 1:5; 3:5, 15). As we honor Him in our hearts and homes, so also we will honor Him in the congregation.

Having considered some of the challenges for leadership, we now will consider what is involved in the process of developing leaders.

## DEVELOPMENT PROCESS: TARP

TARP is a four-fold process of leader-making. The "**T**" stands for task, "**A**" for assistance, "**R**" for responsibility, and "**P**" for position.

### TASK

A task is an activity of work to be accomplished around the congregation. Eventually a person will need to understand how and why a task is attempted. First, however, they need to be willing do the task itself. A task orients the individual to the actual work being done. That is the first step.

NOTES:

For illustration purposes, let's use an example of setting up the chairs for weekly service to see how the development process works from a task to a leadership position. I would like the chairs set up in a certain way, which is not obvious or intuitive to all. In our communities we want to be focusing on the Word of God so we have the chairs all facing to the front, and the aisles may be a certain distance apart. Thus I will probably ask if a person can help me with the task of setting up the chairs.

If this person is willing to help with the task, then it is my responsibility to be clear and direct on what is needed. People expect clear instruction at the start of their work. They need direction in their tasks. The leader has to be able to direct people both in regard to what needs to be accomplished and how it is to be accomplished.

At this level, if the individual will not heed direct instruction, then he may not have the right attitude for training. Perhaps he lacks motivation to participate, or feels he is above taking instructions. The yielded attitude is essential, not the assumed wisdom to accomplish the task; that wisdom will come in time if the attitude is right. The Scriptures tells us that "the fear of the Lord is the beginning of wisdom" (Psalm 111:10). Wisdom is the result of the proper attitude.

In some cases, leadership development can also break down because leaders are not direct. They may be afraid of offending or making people uncomfortable, so they do not give clear directions for carrying out tasks. Providing proper orientation prevents tasks from being handled haphazardly.

NOTES:

## ASSISTANCE

Assistance means that a trainee regularly helps accomplish the ministry. At this stage, they will need to have the work explained in more detail.

If the individual was responsive to direction and orientation, I will ask the person then to assist me on a regular basis. If the person agrees, I might find myself with someone who can be an assistant. However, it is important not to rush through this assistant phase. The trainee must be given time to "feel it out." As they begin taking things a bit more seriously, they may start asking questions. "Why do we set the chairs up this way? Why don't we put them all in a circle?" These questions are encouraged at this stage.

I might explain that it is set up in such a way because we want everyone to be facing toward the Word of God. Or perhaps the chairs are spaced up this way because we need to have enough room to allow for people to come and go. At this stage, the leader is to be ready to share the reasons and the values which underlie the activity.

The person who is assisting may not be able to progress as an assistant if he cannot commit to regular service, as well as understand the task in which he is involved in. By considering the task and why it is meaningful for the life of the congregation, he will grow in his (or her) leadership development.

For his part, the leader has to be thorough. Development requires investing in people who will understand values behind our behaviors and service; we do not expect a congregation of robots. Rather, questions should be encouraged and not seen as threatening. Good leaders seek to teach their values through service.

## RESPONSIBILITY

It is our desire to see people not merely do regular tasks, but also to take on responsibilities of handling those tasks. In this way servants mature as they apply the truth to their lives in their service for Him. Participation and creativity are essential for continued spiritual growth at this stage.

If a person is regularly assisting in setting up chairs, then I might eventually ask them if he would like to assist me further and handle the responsibility himself. If I am away or busy with another responsibility, for example, he will be responsible for setting up chairs.

As an assistant takes on the responsibility, I will be more interested in his ideas on how to accomplish the activity more effectively or more efficiently. After all, the setting up of chairs could potentially be completed in a variety of ways as long as the same values are being consistently demonstrated.

If he understands the values behind the activity and is responsible for the task to get done, he is to be empowered to implement changes. However, balance is needed so any change in the way the activity is conducted must not imply a change in values. A growing servant should want his creativity reflecting to the values of Scripture. Biblical values should be lived out even as our culture changes. Pray that the Lord gives trainees creativity which stem from the right attitude, values, and commitment to the work.

Leaders must be prepared to encourage innovation and evaluate, together with the trainee the effect of those changes. They are to recognize together that proposed changes to the activities do not imply a change in the congregation's values. Without creativity, the community will fossilize over time. The leader at this stage is like a cheerleader, looking to encourage and inspire people who can find new ways of conducting ministry and service. In this way we are more effective in glorifying God and reaching out to lost people as we build up the body of Messiah.

NOTES:

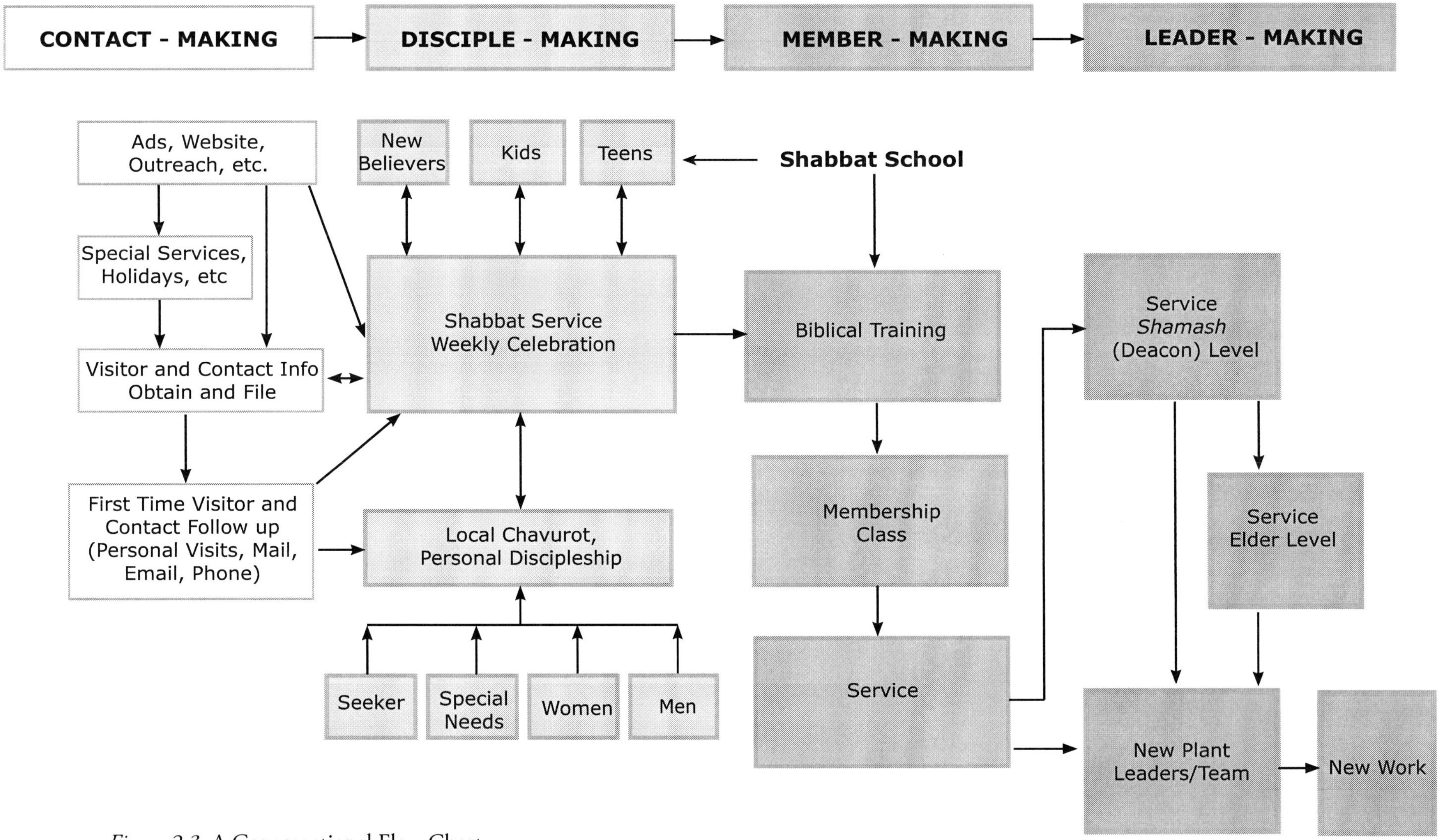


*Figure 2.3.* A Congregational Flow Chart

## POSITION

Lastly, definitely lastly, is the issue of position. At this point, the trainee is being delegated a leadership role in the congregation.

If someone has shown faithfulness in the responsibility of setting up chairs, and has participated in developing and refining the tasks showing that he understands the values, eventually I seek to give him the position of "chairman" (or to whatever position this process applies).

Two levels of positional leadership are described in the Scriptures: *shamash* (servant, or "deacon") and *zaken* ("elder"). The responsibilities can be seen in 1 Timothy 3. An individual should not be made a *shamash* unless they have already demonstrated faithfulness in service. Someone should not be made an elder until they have shown wisdom, counsel, and clear direction in the Word of God for the community and congregation. Ideally people should say, "Wasn't he already an elder? I sure thought he was." This is because he has faithfully comported himself to the responsibilities of ministry, with the same dedication as if he had the position.

The trained person may fail at this point if they get focused on their new title or authority. Titles are necessary only so people know who to be referred to for a particular need, but they are the last thing to consider. Someone who is given a title must continue to rely on *Ruach HaKodesh* for empowerment.

The trainer now must understand that delegating eventuates in not only the responsibility, but also the position transitioning to a new person. He must be steady toward this new leader with encouragement and counsel, and also be willing to cut the apron strings when appropriate. This newly trained person is then able to recruit and train others who can be directed in the task, understand the values behind it, and take on this service as a responsibility. Ideally, a leader with a new position already has someone who he has been training and who is now assisting him.

Let us review some of the issues for the development of leaders in a Messianic congregation. First, there has to be vision and philosophy for leadership. There must be a vision in order for everyone to grow into leadership, starting with their own lives. All are to be Spirit-led, beginning with our families. We have to take responsibility for the ministry in our homes before we try to apply the values in the congregation.

Then there is process training of members in leadership development. There will be need to have classes established for this training, so that people who

NOTES:

help with responsibilities will be ready to raise up others. There is a need for encouragement and also correction. Good people need course correction. People need to grow in a helpful and healthy fashion.

Finally, there is the recognition of delegated responsibilities. It needs to be understood in the congregation which people have been recognized as leaders in the community, so that no one has to guess where the responsible lies. There needs to be ongoing encouragement and further training in leadership as well (See Figure 2.4).

| **Steps** | **Initial** → | **Investing** → | **Growth** → | **Maturity** |
|---|---|---|---|---|
| ***For Trainer*** | **Be Direct** | **Be Accurate** | **Be Creative** | **Be Steady** |
| ***For Trainee*** | **Orientation** | **Explanation** | **Participation** | **Delegation** |
| ***Activity*** | **Task** | **Assistance** | **Responsibility** | **Position** |

*Figure 2.4* Leadership Development Process

NOTES:

## TEACHING THE WORD

We have considered the structure of the ministry of the Word by looking at its four systems. These systems lead to contacts, disciples, members, and leaders who keep a congregation functioning.

However, the content of the ministry of the Word is the Word itself. Thus, it is necessary for us to briefly consider the matter of teaching in the congregation.

Some think of teaching as an activity only for those of a certain class or gifting. However, even as all believers in Messiah are to be followers of Messiah and Spirit-led, so also all followers are to be, in some respect, teachers (Hebrews 5:12). We can easily see how this applies to those who have children (Deuteronomy 6:7). However, even single men and women are called to make disciples (Matthew 28:19-20). Yet, Jacob says, "let not all of you be teachers, knowing that as such we will incur stricter judgment" (James 3:1). Thus, we are called to provide not just any sort of teaching, but to provide sound teaching. King Solomon presents a key passage on this point:

> In addition to being a wise man, the Preacher also taught the people knowledge; and he pondered, searched out and arranged many proverbs.

> The Preacher sought to find delightful words and to write words of truth correctly. The words of wise men are like goads, and masters of these collections are like well-driven nails; they are given by one Shepherd. But beyond this, my son, be warned: the writing of many books is endless, and excessive devotion to books is wearying to the body. (Ecclesiastes 12:9-12)

It is true that life under the sun is complete vanity. Nevertheless, we are called to bring the Creator's redemption into this world. An essential means of bringing His redemption is through sound teaching of His revelation. This passage gives us a methodology for doing so, in preparation (v. 9), presentation (10), appropriation (11), and finally limitation (12).

## PREPARATION (ECCLESIASTES 12:9)

> In addition to being a wise man, the Preacher also taught the people knowledge. (Ecclesiastes 12:9a)

*Kohelet (the Preacher) was wise.* The word for "wise" is *chacham.* Wisdom is the application of God's word to our lives; the wise are skillfully applying His truth as they live. Biblical wisdom was to live out the word of God.

*The teacher must be wise himself.* This is the beginning not the goal of growth. Having wisdom must precede good teaching, just as having money precedes benevolence. The author Solomon, in spite of personal failings, must have retained the gift of wisdom, which he had asked for and obtained for the benefit of his people (Proverbs 2:9; cf. 1 Kings 3:9-12; 4:29-34).

NOTES:

He also taught the people knowledge. If a teacher is only wise for himself, he is not truly wise at all. The activity of teaching is the highest work of service (1 Timothy 5:17). Those taught are not necessarily the powerful, the wealthy, or the intellectual class. Yeshua died for all people; we minister to the same. Prepare teaching, not merely for professors and scholars, but for *am ha-aretz,* the common people. The object is "knowledge," or truth, which is God's word and life (Hosea 4:6; Romans 10:3). A teacher is not a miser in accumulating knowledge; instead he is to use knowledge for the benefit of others. He taught others with full regard for his responsibility as one authorized to do so. The idea was to know by experience (*yadah*). Thus he was giving them insight for living, not just information with no practical results.

Those taught should not be dependent on the teacher, but on the Lord. Taught *(limad)* is from the same root as learned (*lamad*): it literally means "to cause to learn," or facilitate learning. To bring about wisdom for living in others is greater than giving them the correct answers, the difference between giving a man a fish and teaching him how to fish.

*Limad* has the idea of training as well as educating (this aspect can be seen in the derived term for "ox goad," *malmad*, in Hosea 10:11). To learn is to come to terms with the will and law of God.

> ... he pondered, and sought out, and set in order many proverbs. (Ecclesiastes 12:9b)

The Kohelet *pondered.* He was observing the text carefully (Psalm 1:2-3; Joshua 1:7-8). This implies thinking deeply and considering it, deliberating about the meaning of the words. Grammar and context matter profoundly in discovering what a text means.

The word "pondered" (*izen*) comes from "ear" or "hearing." Representing hearing and obedience, the ear is involved in important symbolic actions. If a slave chose to serve his master permanently, his ear was pierced with an awl (Exodus 21:6; Deuteronomy 15:17; cf. Psalm 40:6). By this legal act, the slave was bound to obedience for his entire life. At the ordination of Aaron and his sons to the priesthood, some blood from the sacrificial ram was placed on the lobes of their right ears (as well as their thumbs and big toes, Leviticus 8:23-24; Exodus 29:20). Consideration of the Master's words proves submission to the Master. Rather than take the words to mean whatever feels right to us, or to imply whatever we needed to make our point, we submit to the meaning of the text.

NOTES:

*He sought out.* He delved deeply for truths to be found in the text (2 Timothy 2:15). Questions were his flashlight, which looked into the depths of the truth. "Searched out" (*chiker*) has the idea of "investigate" or "examine." It can refer to initial phases of a search or the end result (which in studying a passage will reveal its *theme),* but always connotes a diligent probing. This word is used concerning investigating legal cases (Proverbs 18:17), the plight of the needy (Job 29:16), searching out a particular subject (Job 5:27; 8:8; 28:27). The work of preparation is difficult and involves diligent research.

He set in order. The Hebrew *tiken* means to "make straight." He arranged, or outlined. The idea of an outline is not to set limits on the truth in the text itself. There is always more than can ever be observed, let alone outlined! Rather, through outlining, the things the student has learned becomes accessible, both for himself (or herself), and others.

Organization is like making a map of the new truth territory we have discovered, so that the teacher might find his way back again, and bring others with him. In reality, one cannot teach everything found in the text. The insights have to be prioritized according to the theme, which is what the text as a whole is saying.

Proverbs (*meshalim*) are wise instructions, which represented truth in an applicable form. The Hebrew for proverb (*mashal*) is from the root to represent, be like or to compare. We study the word so that the truth might be proverbial in people's lives.

## PRESENTATION (V. 10)

When presenting a message, I counsel preachers to consider four aspects to each of the points they wish to make: 1) explanation, 2) illustration, 3) application, and 4) exhortation.

> The Kohelet sought to find delightful words and to write words of truth correctly. (Ecclesiastes 12:10)

*Delightful words* are not only practical, but creatively presented. We seek to communicate effectively so as to impart to others the spiritual nourishment we have already received from the Word (1 Timothy 4:6). Taking care to find the fitting word is pleasurable and meaningful. "Like apples of gold in settings of silver is a word spoken in right circumstances" (Proverbs 25:11).

Again, he *sought to find (baqash)* delightful words, seeking as a shepherd would seek after lost sheep (Psalm 119:176). To find is to discover and take hold of, to grasp to apprehend, even to conquer. This work is like finding a needle in a haystack. The right word and illustration communicates perfectly what the many wrong words will never do.

NOTES:

Accurate words are:

- ***Written** (katuv)* to objectify the truth. They are worth recording and marking down, getting out on paper (papyrus, or a word processor, or what have you).
- ***Words of truth*** (*div'rei emet*), in that they reflect the character of God. The Lord says, "let him who has My word speak My word in truth (Jeremiah 23:28).
- ***Presented correctly*** (*yoshar),* as in accurate as possible to God's will. This refers to straightness and uprightness in one's explanation. Yes, accuracy (the godly teacher), clarity (the good teacher), and creativity (the great teacher) make up a teacher of the Word; but before all there must be accuracy. Now, this certainly does not mean he confused truth with dullness (10a). Rather, he wrote "in an attractive style" (JB). However, accuracy must not be traded in for creativity (2 Timothy 2:15).

## APPROPRIATION (V. 11)

> The words of the wise men are like goads, and masters of these collections are like well-driven nails; they are given by one Shepherd. (Ecclesiastes 12:11)

This is about getting the ball across the goal line: the results of the word (application and exhortation)

***Intensify:*** They motivate to live faithfully, like a farmer's goads: sharp sticks that farmers use to motivate the ox to pull the plow. They provoke others unto love and good deeds (Hebrews 10:24). Wise teachings are to goad their readers to action.

***Clarify:*** They focus to live steadfastly –like a carpenter's well-driven nails. The teaching should stabilize them to persevere in God's word throughout life: To master (*Baali)* is to possess, own. The collected wise words of God (the Scriptures) are integrated into the teacher's soul, as part of his value system and thought process. Those who have mastered these collections of wisdom are like well-driven firmly established nails. Once I was helping a contractor friend build a store. When he saw me hammering, he commented "Sam, your hammering is like lightning—you never hit the same spot twice." We want to avoid the crooked nails which result from such hammering. Teaching from the *bema* is to incisively and decisively speak the truth in love and refute the gainsayers. Masters of these collections are founded upon the rock (Matthew 7:24-25). They help the *talmidim* to be planted by living waters and firmly established in the truth (Psalm 1:2-3).

NOTES:

***Glorify:*** They unify to live agreeably, like a shepherd gathering a flock. The teaching should gather them to follow the One Shepherd forever. A master is a mature teacher of the word who rightly divides the word of truth. There may be many masters, but there is only One Shepherd. All masters learn the truth of His Word; therefore all glorify the One Shepherd (Chagigah 3b).

We are to convey His values and vision to the flock. Proverbs, Isaiah, Deuteronomy, Mark, Revelation—all are from One Shepherd. If the flock is to move forward in unity, He alone can be our focus. The wise draw their wisdom from the Shepherd of Israel, the one true God (Genesis 49:24; Psalm 23:1; 80:1).

## LIMITATION (V. 12)

> But beyond this, my son, be warned: the writing of many books is endless, and excessive devotion to books is wearying to the body. (Ecclesiastes 12:12)

*The work is not to be endless.* Land the plane! Beyond this, beyond the practical and edifying ministry of teaching people the truth of God, there lies vanity.

*Writing of many books is endless:* understand there's much more which could be done; you can write books endlessly. Let us not make writing books a goal itself —this is vain conceit, anything other than what helps us to rejoice in and obey God is vanity (12:13-14). Do not go further than what is useful and profitable for the people. Being a writer without application is endless; such people never get anywhere ("ever learning but never coming to the knowledge of the truth" 2 Tim 3:7). Limitation provides focus, fulfillment, and closure.

*The work is not to be exhausting:* study for application. Great study is a labor for the flesh. There is hard work in teaching (1 Timothy 5:17). Devotion is good and needed; but to be excessive is enervating to the soul, not spiritually energizing. As the Lord loves a cheerful giver, so once it gets beyond cheerful, stop giving! The goal of learning is living and giving, not learning for its own sake.

The teacher must keep his eye on the ball. The goal of ministry is to help and encourage people to obey God and follow His word (Ecclesiastes 12:13). Everything will be evaluated and judged according to truth of God's word whether or not it accomplished the purposes of God (Ecclesiastes 12:14; 1 Timothy 1:4).

## Chapter 8

# Overseer and Admin

We have looked at two of the three main responsibilities of Messianic congregational work, which are founded on the three main ministries of Yeshua. These are Prayer (living out the work of Yeshua as our *Kohen Gadol*) and the Ministry of the Word (living out the work of Yeshua as the true Prophet as exhibited by Moses). Now the final responsibility to consider is overseer, living out Messiah as King.

The responsibility of overseer includes the work of administration and management. It is easy to dismiss administration as a leadership role; it generally takes place behind the scenes, and is nearly invisible when successful. However, administration is vital in that it provides stability, proper encouragement and health to the congregation. The point of overseer and its administration is to ensure the responsibilities, such as prayer and ministry of the Word are carried out well, which thereby provides the actual fellowship (participating in body life) of the congregation.

A flock needs spiritual oversight. The word for the gift of "administration" (*kubernesis)* is only used once in the New Covenant (1 Corinthians 12:28), and a word from the same root is used to speak of the pilot of a ship (Acts 27:11; James 3:4). That's a good metaphor for our purposes. The captain (overseer) understands and sets the strategic goals; the pilot (administrator) helps get us there.

Administration helps the congregation to implement resources properly. It provides the structure, like a skeleton for muscle. Muscles need a skeleton to be upright and the skeleton needs muscle to get somewhere. Elder-led administration keeps a congregation upright and with a structure. The effect of this ministry is to provide the fellowship of the congregation, to achieve the very goals God has called us to achieve.

## The Office of Overseer

The book of Acts first describes the establishment of the congregation in chapters 1-5, and then, the focus of the book shifts in chapters 6-11 as the original leaders (*Shlichim*, the Apostles) are empowering other leaders through delegation. Following this through the rest of the book, local leadership takes over and the original leaders leave the scene. Let us focus on where delegation first becomes an issue in Acts 6.

> Now in these days when the disciples were increasing in number, a complaint by the Hellenists arose against the Hebrews because their widows were being neglected in the daily distribution. (Acts 6:1)

The widows among the "Hellenists," or Greek-speaking Jews, were not getting fed in the daily distribution of food and therefore the Greek believers became a bit upset over it. Their complaint was brought to the leadership in Jerusalem. In their response, we see three matters which are vital for the ministry of overseer.

### Prioritization of the Work

> So the twelve summoned the congregation of the disciples and said, "It is not desirable for us to neglect the word of God in order to serve tables. (Acts 6:2)

The Word is priority. The leadership in Jerusalem gives a surprising response: "It is not desirable for us to neglect the Word of God in order to serve tables" (Acts 6:2). The Apostles prioritized serving the Word over serving tables. Proper prioritization of what is strategically important is the first work of an overseer.

Overseers set the priorities. Who sets the priorities in the home? It is the parents, those entrusted with overseeing. The same rule applies in the congregation. Those entrusted with overseeing the work set the priorities. Moreover, we see precisely what priorities the overseers set: "prayer and the ministry of the word" (Acts 6:4). These are the same priorities which are to be set in the congregation (and home) today.

### DELEGATION IN THE WORK

> Therefore, brethren, select from among you seven men of good reputation, full of the Spirit and of wisdom, whom we may put in charge of this task. (Acts 6:3a)

The vision is greater than you. Though it was not their priority, the leaders did not leave the problem without a solution. They did not dismiss the problem out of hand ("Oh well, I guess God wants your widows to fast!"). Nor did they bother speculating as to whether the complaint was motivated by a rebellious critical spirit. Rather, they recognized the need itself, and also that they would require others to help them to address the need.

The Apostles showed trust to those Greek-speaking Jews and told them to find seven men of good reputation, filled with the Spirit and wisdom. It was clear that the work would extend beyond their sphere. Prioritization leads to delegation. Once you have the priorities, then you can delegate in accordance with those priorities. We need to delegate so that the work of God is accomplished.

### SUPERVISION OF THE WORK OF GOD

It goes on to say:

> Select from you seven men of good reputation, full of the Spirit and of wisdom whom we may put in charge of this task... The statement found approval with the whole congregation; and they chose Stephen, a man full of faith and of the Holy Spirit, and Philip, and Prochorus, and Nicanor, and Timon, and Parmenas, and Nicolaus, a proselyte of Antioch. These they set before the apostles, and they prayed and laid their hands on them. (Acts 6:3, 5-6)

NOTES:

All of those selected have Greek names, which makes sense since they worked in the Greek speaking Jewish community of Jerusalem where the Good News was spreading. By laying hands on them, the Apostles were publicly recognizing their calling and their responsibility. Though the ones who brought the complaint selected them, the men chosen would then report to the apostolic leadership. In other words, the Apostles would supervise them.

A reporting system helps evaluate progress. The first aspect of overseer is prioritization; the second is delegation; and, the third is supervision. There needs to be a reporting system for the benefit of all. Remember, people do not always do what is expected, but what is inspected. Through proper supervision there can be mutual, loving accountability in the congregation and in the community.

## Overseer office in the Torah

This three-fold responsibility of overseer is found not only here but throughout the work of God. In Exodus 18, Moses has a visit from his father-in-law Jethro, who gives Moses some advice and counsel. He sees Moses working day and night but he is concerned that it will not be helpful. He says to Moses, "The thing you are doing is not good" (Exodus 18:17).

Imagine saying to Moses that what he is doing is *lo tov,* "not good." That takes some gumption. Jethro says in verse 18, "You will surely wear out, both yourself and these people who are with you..."

There were only two things wrong with what Moses was doing: it would kill him, and it would kill the people. The reason was that "the task is too heavy for you; you cannot do it alone" (18:18). Jethro goes on to say to Moses:

> Now listen to me: I will give you counsel, and God be with you. You be the people's representative before God, and you bring the disputes to God... Stand before God for the people, so that you may bring the difficulties to God. (Exodus 18:19)

*The first matter was to be prayer.* Moses was to intercede before the Lord and pray on these matters. Next, Jethro says to Moses:

> And you shall teach them the statutes and the laws, and show them the way in which they must walk and the work they must do. (Exodus 18:20)

NOTES:

*We see here the ministry of the Word.* Moses was to teach God's instructions and how it applies to their lives, not only the inspirational truth but also the application for their lives. Jethro goes on to say:

> Moreover you shall select from all the people able men, such as fear God, men of truth, hating covetousness; and place such over them to be rulers of thousands, rulers of hundreds, rulers of fifties, ruler of tens. And let them judge the people at all times. Then it will be that every great matter they shall bring to you, but every small matter they themselves shall judge. So it will be easier for you for they will bear the burden with you. (Exodus 18:20-21)

Various levels of leadership are involved here. Note also that the rulers are delegated their authority and supervised by Moses.

These same three aspects found in Acts 6 are also found in the counsel of Jethro to Moses, pray, teach and oversee. These three elements are fundamental to the proper functioning of the congregation: prayer, the ministry of the Word, and overseer. Moreover, in the Exodus text as well, the overseer sets the priorities, delegates, and supervises accordingly to make sure the work is done.

## Overseeing and Fellowship

One of the purposes of a congregation is to be a center for fellowship. However, the word fellowship is often used in a lax way to mean two people hanging out together, as in going to the movies together or "just hanging out" counting as fellowship. What is the ministry of fellowship (*haverut*; *koinonia*) as it is taught in the Word of God? *Koinonia* is from the root of common; it has to with what we hold in common. If an Oxford graduate with a degree in Shakespeare would be invited to join the Shakespeare fellowship, what would they talk about? And if the person was more interested in rugby, he could join the rugby team. Now after the Shakespeare Fellowship adjourns, some may go to the rugby match; but they would not be there as part of the proceedings of the Shakespeare fellowship. In the Bible the word is used in such a way. Believers have Yeshua in common; thus, our fellowship is about Him. We have fellowship in our priorities not our secondary matters (except when they are used to express the primary matters).

### The Character of Fellowship

Its character of fellowship is spiritual relationships, in two senses. First, we have fellowship in the Lord:

> God is faithful, through whom you were called into fellowship with His Son, Yeshua Messiah our Lord. (1 Corinthians 1:9)

> That I may know Him and the power of His resurrection and the fellowship of His sufferings, being conformed to His death. (Philippians 3:10)

> I pray that the fellowship of your faith may become effective through the knowledge of every good thing which is in you for Messiah's sake. (Philemon 1:6)

> ... what we have seen and heard we proclaim to you also, so that you too may have fellowship with us; and indeed our fellowship is with the Father, and with His Son Yeshua the Messiah... If we say that we have fellowship with Him and yet walk in the darkness, we lie and do not practice the truth; but if we walk in the Light as He Himself is in the Light, we have fellowship with one another, and the blood of Yeshua His Son cleanses us from all sin. (1 John 1:3; 6-7)

> The grace of the Lord Yeshua the Messiah, and the love of God, and the fellowship of the Holy Spirit, be with you all. (2 Corinthians 13:14)

Our fellowship is essentially fellowship with the Lord, but also in Him (abiding in Him).

Second, our fellowship is with the Lord's people:

> Do not be bound together with unbelievers; for what partnership have righteousness and lawlessness, or what fellowship has light with darkness? (2 Corinthians 6:14)

> Therefore if there is any encouragement in Messiah, if there is any consolation of love, if there is any fellowship of the Spirit, if any affection and compassion, make my joy complete by being of the same mind, maintaining the same love, united in Spirit, intent on one purpose. (Philippians 2:1-2)

Our fellowship together is found with and among believers in Yeshua.

### THE ACTIVITIES OF FELLOWSHIP

The activities of fellowship are seen through the three primary responsibilities of the Messianic congregation: worship, ministry of the Word, and overseer (Acts 6:1-7; Exodus 18:18-22). Our fellowship of worship is in praising the Lord together.

> We who had sweet fellowship together walked in the house of God in the throng. (Psalms 55:14)

> Is not the cup of blessing which we bless a sharing (*koinonia*) in the blood of Messiah? Is not the bread which we break a sharing in the body of Messiah? (1 Corinthians 10:16)

Together in fellowship, we worship the Lord as a community. Worship of the one God binds us together in fellowship.

Our fellowship of the Word is in study, learning, witness, and mission:

> ...and recognizing the grace that had been given to me, Jacob and Cephas and John, who were reputed to be pillars, gave to me and Barnabas the right hand of fellowship, so that we might go to the Gentiles and they to the circumcised. (Galatians 2:9)

NOTES:

> ...in view of your participation (*koinonia*) in the gospel from the first day until now. (Philippians 1:5)
>
> They were continually devoting themselves to the apostles' teaching and to fellowship, to the breaking of bread and to prayer. (Acts 2:42)

Together in fellowship, we witness, edify one another in teaching, and help advance the Good News in our relationships and testimony.

Our fellowship in administration/overseer is found in support: helping each other, extending benevolence and mercy.

> For Macedonia and Achaia have been pleased to make a contribution (*koinonia*) for the poor among the saints in Jerusalem. (Romans 15:26)
>
> ...begging us with much urging for the favor of participation (*koinonia*) in the support of the saints, ... Because of the proof given by this ministry, they will glorify God for your obedience to your confession of the gospel of Messiah and for the liberality of your contribution to them and to all. (2 Corinthians 8:4; 9:13)
>
> And do not neglect doing good and sharing, for with such sacrifices God is pleased. When together in fellowship we help and care for each other in an orderly way. (Hebrews 13:16)

NOTES:

This does not mean there is a problem with bowling, movies, Super Bowl parties, or going out for coffee. However, when it comes to setting the priorities, delegating, and supervising activities of fellowship, the overseers must act as wise adults (Ephesians 4:29). Apart from worship, ministry of the Word, or overseeing and administrations of mercy to the flock, such things may not qualify as matters of genuine spiritual fellowship for the congregation.

Various events may have value for outreach, prayer, or ministering to needs; otherwise they are secondary matters, which may not need to take up the focus of a congregation. In scheduling "fellowship ministry," if it does not further the real purposes of a congregation, it should be understood as personal activity.

Keeping our eyes on the priorities of Messianic ministry is essential to accomplishing the work. We have now seen the structure and systems of a Messianic congregation in light of the three responsibilities of Messianic ministry: prayer, ministry of the Word, and overseer (*see Figure 2.5*). These responsibilities are for the Body of Messiah, in which they might, in its fullness reflect the threefold-work of Messiah Himself.

| Ministries/ Systems | Contact-Making | Disciple-Making | Member-Making | Leader-Making |
|---|---|---|---|---|
| **Worship** | Praying for and with contacts | Training believers in prayer and worship | Members are praying for each other's needs and worshipping in unity. | Leading in public prayer and worship. |
| **Ministry of the Word** | Evangelization: Proclaim the Word of salvation | Edification: Teach believers to study and memorize Scripture. | Edification: Train and evaluate disciples on values theology, and beliefs. | Edification: Training and Coaching for Ministry of the Word. |
| **Overseer** | Organize Finding, File and Follow-up outreach. | Organize opportunities for public and small group growth. | Organize membership classes, training for immersion, evaluations, member service and care. | Appoint elders and *shamashim*. |

*Figure 2.5*: Ministry Responsibilities and System Matrix

# PART 3

# PLANNING MESSIANIC CONGREGATIONS

## Chapter 9

# How to Plan for Congregational Development

Part 1 addressed the characteristics, values, and vision needed for a planter and his core group. Part 2 then showed the Biblical responsibilities and systems of a Messianic congregation plant. Now, in Part 3, we will look closely at the planning process. First, we will consider the general principles of planning and then consider again a general plan or schedule for planting a Messianic congregation.

Planning is a decision-making process by which ministries develop their objectives, strategies, and action plans in order to achieve them. Planning emphasizes present decisions which affect future activities and results. When leaders are pro-active in planning for their responsibilities, they are more likely to be effective, and less likely to be merely reactive to the problems which inevitably arise.

An interesting, edifying, and educational study on planning can be found in Paul's year-long travel plans (1 Corinthians 16:3-9), which extended in his letter to the believers at Rome (Romans 15:15-29), comparing how it worked out for him in Luke's account (Acts 19-21). Even though a *shaliach* (apostle), Paul still had to plan. In fact, because he was mature, he knew the importance of planning to properly utilize the limited resources available to accomplish the work of HaShem. And though he planned well, he still was wise enough to say, "If the Lord permits" (1 Corinthians 16:7), as he knew only HaShem is Lord over our assumptions. We will touch on these matters later on in our considerations of the planning process.

## Planning Preliminaries

Although there may not be much thought given to planning, it is a commonplace kind of thing. We all do it. Suppose I need to go to the store. I would have to address these things: Where do I have to go? Where am I now? How do I get from here to there? That is a plan. It may be almost automatic, not given any consideration. However, when it comes to planting a congregation, thought and intentionality should be given to the planning process. There are some preliminaries requiring consideration.

***Why Do We Plan?*** We plan, first of all, in order to be good stewards of God's resources. We want to get to where God has called us. Planning consists of decisions to utilize ministry resources to accomplish ministry goals. Resources include finances, and also people's time and abilities. In this regard, there is a deeper reason for good planning. Leaders have a stewardship to promote unity and trust within the congregation. How do we achieve that unity and trust in the ministry of the congregation? Planning develops this unity and trust in the congregation, by bringing people on board regarding what we are attempting to accomplish.

***Who Gets To Plan?*** Those involved in the planning process should be responsible for carrying out the activities. They share the vision and implementation, and so will be impacted by the plan. Even if they are not involved in the actual planning meetings as such they can still be communicated with and brought in at some level. By the same token, it can be distracting when people who are not committed to the goals and values of the congregation end up as part of the planning team.

***When Do We Get to Plan?*** This needs to happen when there is a vision from God and an understanding of the situation. Nehemiah's planning process can give some insight (Nehemiah 2:12-19). First he received what the Lord wanted him to do. Then, he evaluated the extent of the problem to be fixed. Finally, he discussed the plan with the community in Jerusalem. One cannot plan further than the clarity of the vision, nor beyond the resources that the Lord has provided. The vision becomes the ultimate goal of the planning process.

***What Do We Plan?*** We plan for manageable objectives which fulfill the vision and goals of a Messianic synagogue. Initially, we plan how to recruit for a core group and other preliminary matters; then with the core group, we plan to have a functional congregation plant (and even a consecration service); then we plan for the development of the congregation, including leadership development; and then we plan to stay healthy and reproduce as a mature congregation.

Leaders, as the overseers of the flock of the Lord, should keep in mind three main and ongoing responsibilities with respect to communicating and managing these planned objectives with a goal of promoting unity and trust within the group.

*Firstly, encourage people in how God is blessing their ministry.* It may be that the enemy would have pushed the group back a mile, whereas in fact, we gained a whole inch of territory for the Lord. This is no small thing to encourage. Leadership evaluates properly, so that the group can celebrate what the Lord has done.

*Secondly, reiterate what the vision is and the goals in light of that vision.* We always want to keep our planning, achievements, and successes tied to the vision.

*Thirdly, in light of the vision, lead in planning further manageable objectives to achieve the vision.* The vision itself encourages us to do "our utmost for His highest" and that should equate to practical objectives to further the Good News, build up His people, and glorify His name.

Though the Lord gives the increase, the way in which a leader contributes to the growth of a Messianic synagogue is by pointing to Yeshua and encouraging others in Him. We should be diligent to make sure that our objectives reflect that which is of primary importance (Figure 3.0).

NOTES:

**OBJECTIVES IN PLANNING**

**Luke 14:28-32; Acts 9:10-16; Philippians 3:12-14**

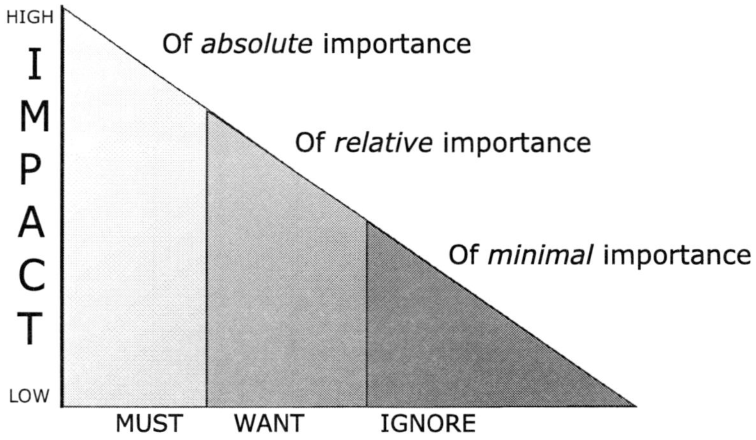


We noted before that planning is done automatically in everyday life. However, the more people involved, the less successful intuitive planning becomes. Everyone has to get on the same page so they can arrive together.

Planting Messianic congregations is largely about solving problems. A problem is whatever prevents you from accomplishing your goals and objectives. For example, the fact that it is a rainy day outside may not be a problem, if the inconvenience of the weather does not hinder me from working inside and accomplishing my objectives. Whether something is a problem must be evaluated in light of whether it actually keeps the team from accomplishing its goals. Three problems that need to be considered are about the very aspects of a plan and a lack of clarity on these matters will impede accomplishment:

1. Where do we want to go?
2. Where are we starting from?
3. How do we get from here to there?

***First of all, where do we want to go?*** That is, what exactly do I want to accomplish? The leader may have in mind a particular idea, but those on the team with him may have a different idea. There needs to be clarity on objectives to have unity in service. In light of this, we will look at five principles for setting well defined objectives.

***Secondly, where are we starting from?*** That is, where are we now? What do we have to work with? What are the issues we are currently facing? This is also called a situational analysis.

***Thirdly, how do we get from here to there?*** This is where we develop strategies to utilize the resources that you have available to accomplish your objectives.

The following principles are commonly taught in the business and management world, but they are easily applicable to congregation planning. A congregation is certainly more than a business or corporation, with a higher set of responsibilities, therefore it should not be any less functional than a business or corporation, or set the bar lower for its functionality. Adequate time needs to be spent on each of these in order for all involved to be on the same page because the planning process is a decision-making process.

## Setting Objectives

We want to see a Messianic congregation bring glory to Yeshua, and, indeed, to represent Him in the redemptive work of prayer, ministry of the Word, and overseer. We set objectives in light of the vision. To set about a ministry without concrete objectives is like drawing the target around the arrow.

NOTES:

The better we clearly understand the objectives to be attained the more likely we are to be able to attain them. That's why we need to have SMART objectives: **Specific, Measurable, Agreed upon**, **Reasonable/relevant,** and **Time-related**.

### SPECIFIC

This stresses the need for a specific objective against a more general idea. The objective should be clear and unambiguous, free of clichés. To make goals specific, they must tell a team exactly what is expected, who's involved, where is it going to happen and which attributes are important.

A specific goal will usually answer five "**W**" questions:

- ***What:*** What do I want to accomplish? What exactly will the objective be?
- ***Why:*** Specific reasons, purpose or benefits of accomplishing the goal. This clarifies values, helping everyone understand the correlation between values/beliefs and activity.
- ***Who:*** Who is involved? Who is impacted, and who will be the point person? Because of limited personnel, it is important to clarify this question.
- ***Where:*** Where will this objective be taking place, or what space will be needed for it?
- ***Which:*** Identify requirements, restrictions, and resources. Which resources will be used for the project? Which local laws and restrictions need to be taken into account?

NOTES:

### MEASURABLE

This stresses the need for concrete benchmarks, needed to measure progress toward the attainment of the goal. If a goal is not measurable, it is not possible to know whether a team is making progress toward successful completion. Measuring progress should help a team stay on track, reach its target dates, and experience the joy of achievement in praise to HaShem that spurs the team on to continued effort required to reach the ultimate goal.

A measurable goal will usually answer questions such as: How much? How many? How will I know when it is accomplished? Some objectives imply a need for "critical mass," a certain number of people to successfully accomplish an activity (i.e., have a *minyan*, pay for a building, etc). In regards to just getting started in core group development, I strongly suggest there be at least ten family units (this may include single individuals as well).

### Agreed upon

This stresses the importance of goals that are realistic and attainable as seen by those that are on the team working toward the objective. People have to be on the same page. We need to utilize our resources as aggressively as we can to accomplish our goals, but agreeing on those goals and what resources will be made available. It must also be remembered that we have to focus on what will be most important to the group. Matters of less importance should be set aside; we must focus to resolve only the priority issues which necessitate consensus.

While an agreed objective should stretch a team in order to achieve it, however it should not be extreme. There needs to be a balance between the objective being neither out of reach ("too idealistic") nor below the community's standard ("who'd want to listen to that?"). An agreed upon objective brings the team closer together and therefore more likely to achieve it, developing the attitudes, abilities, skills, and financial capacity to reach them.

All leaders need to see both unity and trust develop from both the planning and performance of the team. An agreed goal will usually answer the 'how' question: how can the goal be accomplished together so we can adapt in unity and trust?

### Reasonable/Relevant

This stresses the importance of making objectives realistic. A realistic objective must be one that the entire team is willing and able to work towards. This is partly so they see it as relevant, helpful, and applicable to their work of service. The objective should make demands on its members, and may end up stretching the group in the process as noted above. But even so, an objective is seen as reasonable if the team believes that it can be accomplished and that it is worth doing—that it will actually move things forward.

When working in a planning meeting it is advisable that the facilitator gets 'buy in' from those in the meeting. That may mean asking each person around the table if they consider the objective realistic and relevant. Some personalities are not quick out of the gate and need to be encouraged to share their thoughts, assured that they will not be aggressed by stronger personalities. The facilitator is to make sure that each person is listened to with due respect, but also that these discussions are not permitted to go on endlessly.

A reasonable goal will usually answer the question: Does this seem reasonable and relevant to us all?

NOTES:

### Time Related

This stresses the importance of keeping goals within a time frame, giving the group a target date. It is natural for a group to dream and then procrastinate, so as to avoid the stress of working towards it. However, a target date or set of dates in the objective helps a team focus their efforts and grounds them in the real world.

One core group I worked with will only do something if they know that on a certain date they will be asked about it. Cramming for an exam is often the only time work is brought into clear focus, just as on a micro level, I have seen men, sitting out in their cars before class, forcing Bible verses into their heart, because they knew that the homework is due. A time-related objective will establish the sense of priority needed to complete the task, without having to be in a real crisis or tragedy.

A time-related objective will usually answer the question: When? What can we do six months from now? What can we do six weeks from now? What can we do today?

A planning meeting will be a place to work through these things rather carefully as we consider the objectives we want to attain. Qualities to look for in an objective are that it is specific, measurable, agreed upon, realistic, and time-related: SMART. That helps us figure out where we are headed with our objectives.

NOTES:

## Situational Analysis

Having a clear idea of an objective, a group must consider also where it is at present, before they consider a strategy to accomplish the objective. We have to understand who we are and what we bring to the table in light of the objectives we wish to accomplish.

Even with clarified objectives, our strategies depend on our starting point. Suppose I want to meet with Bill in the center of the city. He lives on the north side; I'm on the south side. If he asks me which way to go, telling him to go north will not help him even if this is the direction I go. Different starting points require different strategies to get to the desired goal.

Likewise, for us to understand as a congregation how to achieve our objectives (strategies), we need to agree on our starting point. A situational analysis can be identified by the acrostic SWOT, which is an acrostic for **Strengths**, **Weaknesses, Opportunities** and **Threats**. Strengths and weaknesses refer to analyzing the internal resources of the group; opportunities and threats refer to analyzing the external factors that significantly impacts the work you're doing for HaShem.

### Strengths

What are we doing well? What experience do we bring to the table on some of these affairs? Though God is not dependent upon our experience, we may be able to utilize some of that experience for His work.

Here is an example of matters which could be considered: who among us, perhaps, has the knowledge of liturgy, if this would be something of value to our community? Who among us can teach or even preach the Word of God? Who among us can help with children and other things that we may want to accomplish, other systems that may need to be developed?

### Weaknesses

What are we not doing as well? What weaknesses do we need to compensate for? We might want a live worship team—but if we don't have musicians, we may need to utilize recordings in worship.

What are difficulties regarding space and time? There may be some of us who are bi-vocational and have a smaller amount of time to give to a project. Others in the core group may have only a couple of hours a week to give to an activity. Time is a resource which must be handled very well. The Lord asked us to redeem the time not to waste it. We must be exceedingly careful not to take advantage of willing people; burnout hurts the whole team.

### Opportunities and Threats

As the internal issues of strengths and weaknesses need to be clearly understood, so do the external matters of opportunities and threats need to be understood just as well. Opportunities and threats are those matters that are external to the congregation but can impact the proper functioning of the body. Threats may be anything from a changing economy to "anti-missionary" protests outside the building. Opportunities may include local community events, neighborhood buildings that become available, a new bus service, etc. The threats need to be evaluated to how much of a hindrance they will be to the functioning of the synagogue. The opportunities need to be evaluated at how they will be utilized to expand the work of the congregation.

In these discussions I use a white board, power point (to keep our planning on track), large pads and an easel for writing down the ideas and posting them around the room, so we can discuss them as a group.

NOTES:

Part of that discussion might also include how we got where we are. We may need to review some of the decisions that brought us to where we are now. Remember, we not affixing blame, but fixing problems. Where you are now is partly determined by past decisions, just as where you will be in the future will be a result of the decisions you are making now. The group may need to understand some of the history, possibly reviewing the congregational mission statement, which describes why your congregation exists, and what makes it distinct.

## Developing Strategies

Once you have clearly understood the objectives and once you have discussed where you are in your present situation, you can now ask, "How do I go from here to there?" This will entail utilizing the SWOT resources to develop strategies to accomplish the SMART objectives.

I would encourage great patience in this process. As you discuss the strategies you may realize that we need to have certain short term objectives before the team can develop long-term goals. We don't always have the resources we need for the long term objectives. As I've noted before, you cannot plan beyond the resources you actually control.

In developing strategies, we will have thorny hindrances that need to be resolved before we can move forward to actually accomplishing our objectives. It is natural when you consider the strategies you will also discuss the problems that will hinder those strategies. We resolve these thorny issues by using POP. POP is an acrostic for **Problem**, **Options**, and **Plan**.

NOTES:

***First, we discuss the problem.*** By that I mean listing all aspects of the problem, not just aspects that may seem obvious. Only when a problem is fully understood it can be fully resolved. This is necessary because you need to develop a strong strategy that addresses and resolves the problems and accomplishes the objectives. Remember, each of these matters that you are discussing are those that actually hinder you from accomplishing the establishment of the congregation.

***Next, we consider all possible options to address each aspect of the problem.*** This may call for a bit of brainstorming, where we may have to develop some creative approaches to address our particular problems. The particular aspects of your problems will necessitate at least adapting anyone else's solution to fit your circumstance. Be careful of merely using Saul's armor. Your slingshot may be better than his high-tech sword to resolve your problems. In any case, make sure you have reasonable options to address each aspect of the problem.

***Finally, you put together a plan from the best options that resolve all aspects of the problem in order to move forward to accomplish your goals.*** This is your strategy. Putting together those best options to address those problems becomes the strategy to achieve your objectives.

This process can take some time. In some cases I have spent three days with core groups working through these issues. On the first day, we discuss objectives. On the second day we engage in situational analysis. On the third day, we discuss how we get from here to there. At other sessions, I only have a little bit of time to work with the group, whereas we have to focus on primary matters very quickly to produce a few short-term goals. Some plans require more time to create than others.

Keeping minutes can also be important, especially for financial decisions, since it may be a government requirement. It is good in reviewing the plans that the group can look back at the minutes, understand as to how we arrived at certain decisions, and why this plan needed to be implemented.

## Action Plan

It is the implementation of the plan that makes it work. Yeshua said, "If you know these things, blessed are you that do them" (John 13:17). Knowing how to proceed so as to accomplish it, is the work of an action plan. This differs from the previous step of developing strategies since in an action plan the actual resources and deadlines are written out and committed. An action plan is broken down into delegated action steps that accomplish the overall objectives. An action plan answers:

1. Who?
2. Will be doing what?
3. By when?
4. With how much?

No planning session is complete until these three questions are adequately answered.

*First, who is going to be responsible for what will be accomplished?* There should be a name of a "point person" tied to the action item. For example, if we are to have an *oneg* at the *Sukkot* service, who will be responsible to organize it? What will this person be doing? What exactly do they need to do? This is the content of each action step. Here is where the specificity of the objective will be helpful.

NOTES:

*By when do these individuals need to have this accomplished?* What are the time markers for each step in the plan? If a date was agreed upon when the group was setting objectives, this will be included, however there also have to be other markers for other steps in the action plan.

*How many resources will be needed to get this accomplished on time?* Will the point person have a team to help? What is their budget? What space will they use? Do we need tables and chairs?

The delegated individuals are entrusted with the follow-through of the implementation of the plan. I have found that, once the action plans are delegated, it is often better to agree on precisely what needs to be accomplished however leave with the delegated individual as to precisely how the action step will be accomplished (for example, which stores to buy from and which brands of bagels to buy when preparing the oneg). That is why we need to make sure people are on the same page from the outset. We all need to understand that the accomplishing the objectives according to the action plan will establish, improve, and bless the congregation to the glory of God. Three elements go together: responsibility (what they have to do), authority (the means by which they do it), and accountability (who they report to).

## REPORTING SYSTEM

NOTES:

Once action plans are properly delegated, there needs to be proper follow-through and follow up on these responsibilities. This proper follow-up is a reporting system. The final aspect of the process of developing plans is to develop a reporting system to follow up on the plans.

It bears repeating: people don't do what you expect but what you inspect. Therefore, people assigned responsibilities in the action plans should meet back together as a group and report on the plans.

### THE USE OF MEETINGS

The reporting system is the normal process to evaluate the progress of the plans. We looked at the process of planning, but now we want to evaluate the progress of the plans through regularly scheduled meetings. In some cases, reporting can work through the internet or video-conferencing, depending on the people and action plans, though often meetings work better in person. Meetings are scheduled when everyone can be there, and should be held in a place convenient and comfortable for all. Those attending will have to be notified in a timely manner regarding what is expected of them, as well as aware of the agenda items. This way people are treated fairly, wisely, lovingly, and in a straight-forward fashion.

My suggestion is that meetings get scheduled with respect to the progress and timing of the action plan. Monthly meetings are normal, but may need to be held more often. The planter should delegate to someone to handle the administrative scheduling and coordinating for the group.

Of course, no one likes unnecessary or prolong meetings. In regards to the reporting system and the meeting itself, you will want to be focused on what really needs to get done. The general procedure at a meeting is to call the meeting to order, having a time of prayer, reporting on the ministry's progress, and reviewing future responsibilities of the activities. Keeping minutes is always wise, especially if there will be any financial decisions. Everything should be done in a proper fashion and as the law requires.

During this reporting system the group will discuss what went right. Provide appreciation for those that were able to faithfully follow through on their responsibilities. Especially commend those that had to overcome unexpected difficulties in order to accomplish the goal. Leadership is responsible to appreciate the servants that the Lord chose to use. True, no one should be in it to get the glory, and the real appreciation to hear is: "Well done, good and faithful servant," from the One we gladly serve. However, to appreciate and commend faithful workers is in itself a way of honoring the Lord who gives the increase.

We need to show love to each other, especially during meetings. Love is sometimes shown just through listening carefully to the other person and what they have to say and thinking it through, as opposed to merely waiting to jump in with one's own ideas.

NOTES:

### Assumption Shifts

There also needs to be discussion when matters didn't work out as we expected. We make course corrections during reporting meetings to keep the plan moving forward. Remember, the focus is on fixing problems, not affixing blame.

*An assumption is a temporary estimate of a very important probable development which cannot be predicted with accuracy, is subject to no significant control, and will have major impact on future activities and results.* The reason for course correction is because plans are made on reasonable assumptions. For example, we assumed the point person would stay healthy, but he was sick for a week. Or, she was supposed to have time to work on the project, but his boss required extra work from her that week. We assumed a certain store would carry an item, but alas, it's been discontinued. The weather was not supposed to be bad.

Unexpected problems and unforeseen difficulties do come up. These are all assumption shifts.

Assumption shifts happen to everyone. In fact, as we referred to before, we read in James 4:13, "do not say I am to go to the city and make this much money, rather if the Lord wills it..."

God is in charge of all of these assumptions. How do we develop plans and implement them when we really cannot control various assumptions? You can only work with the resources over which you have a stewardship, but there are innumerable things we do not control, including health, the weather, and factors in the community. A team needs to handle assumption shifts within its reporting system. Key to keeping the plan on track is making the smallest changes possible in light of what circumstances have shifted. We address these changes in order (Figure 3.1).

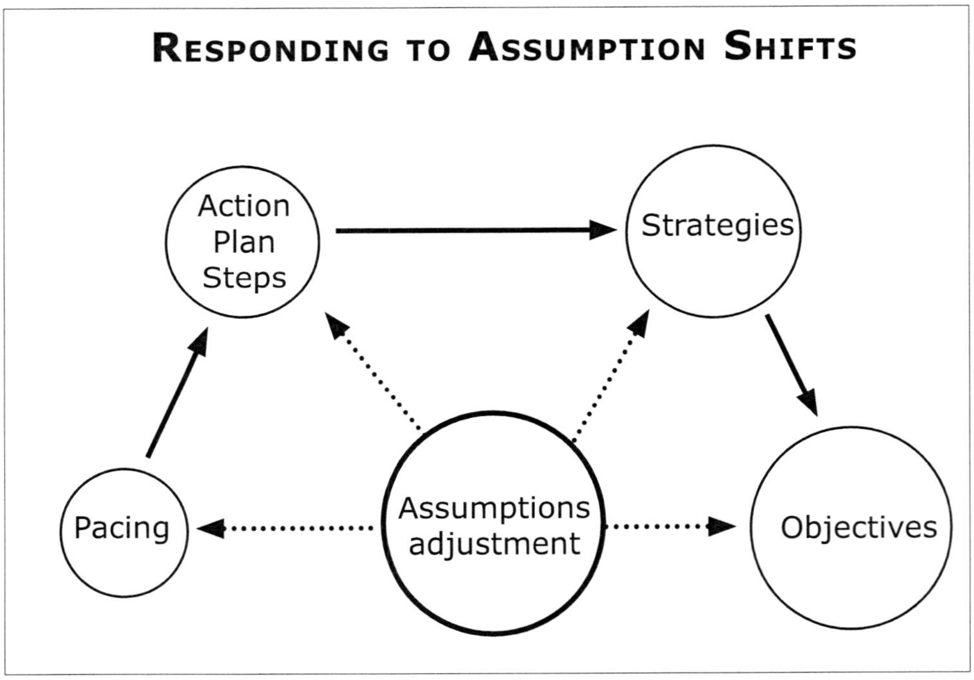


NOTES:

- First, we check to see if the pacing on a plan can be adjusted. We raise such questions as: If we can't do it by Tuesday, then when can we expect that to be accomplished?
- Then, if it's more serious, we see if the steps in the Action Plan need to be adjusted. If Chaim can't make it to set up on Friday, who can be there? What further resources will be needed to accomplish that project? What are the personnel needs we have if it was not done by the assumed people?

- Then, if the assumption shift rules out the Action Plan entirely, the strategies may have to be adjusted. What are some ways we can get back on track regarding that objective? What new approaches do we need to apply to it?

- Only when all other course corrections have been fully considered and ruled out as impossible, only then should changing the objectives themselves enter the discussion. This is because the objectives were set because of their priority for the congregation.

It is possible that the Lord will provide some miracle to replace our stewardship. He is able. However, it is arrogant to plan on miracles instead of planning on what our stewardship requires. The Lord will give the increase (even miraculously), but He has called us "to do the work of service" (Ephesians 4:12). Indeed, "unless the Lord builds the house they who labor, labor in vain" (Psalm 127:1). We are taught to expect to labor, even as we trust Him to do the heavy lifting in building a congregation.

## Adjourning the Meeting

Once course correction has been accomplished, the meeting can go on to other pertinent matters. If nothing else needs to be discussed, we can get ready to adjourn. But first, you'll want to discuss the next meeting date to be scheduled, what will be the results at that meeting that you will be looking for, what needs to be done? The old and new action items will help set the agenda for the next meeting. It is wise to make sure the minutes of the meeting are distributed so all involved can be reminded on what is expected and thereby pray for one another. Everything should be done decently and in order, giving due respect to our brothers and sisters involved.

Let us review the essential steps in the planning process:

1. *Vision and Goals* – what are we are about?
2. *Setting Objectives* – where do we want to go?
3. *Situational Analysis* – where are we now?
4. *Developing Strategies* – how do we get there?
5. *Action Plan* – who will do what by when?
6. *Reporting System* – how are we doing?

For a large, complex organism like a congregation, these are not simple steps, but in fact there will be overlap in how the phases interact. For example, to a

NOTES:

large degree, *Setting Objectives* and *Situational Analysis* will go together, because the specificity, relevance, and timing of the objective towards which the group is aiming depends in part on what its present resources are. Also, as discussed, a situational analysis may include reviewing and reminding each other what the mission is by which the group can evaluate their situation. Through it all, the most important goal for the elders is to see leadership supporting and encouraging one another, growing together in unity and trust. The plans may not succeed or may need eventual revision, but what is most crucial is that the people grow in love one for another. Elders always seek that the plans and programs develop unity and trust in the community.

## Chapter 10

# A Plan for Planting

We have taken a look at the structural vision of a functional and healthy congregation. Functional systems are essential for a healthy congregation. We considered the responsibility of prayer and worship which undergirds the ministry of the Word, and how the overseer's responsibility provides for the functioning of the other two.

We now want to think about the stages in a strategy to realizing a healthy and functioning work of God. This plan or schedule will work together with the planning tools we considered in the previous chapter.

One can think of the schedule and strategy of planting a congregation like having a baby and raising a child. Stages would include: conception, embryonic and fetal stage (*core group development*), birth (*consecration service)*, childhood development, adolescence, and maturity (*leadership development*) (See *figure 3.2* on page 113*)*. Just as a child's body is primarily developed before birth and in the womb, so also we will be focusing on the "pre-birth" phases, which is most relevant to the congregation planter's work.

Understandably, what's presented here is an idealized strategy. Often core-group recruits move to find work in another city, and others may decide this sort of Messianic congregation is not what they were looking for. Not everything works out according to plan, and the actual timing is according to the will of HaShem. However, we are going to look at a congregational planting schedule for a sense of how things proceed.

## INITIAL PHASE

Before there is a congregation, before there may even be the beginnings of a core-group, the planter should get to know the community he is in. One of the things he will be looking to do is to recruit somewhere between ten and fifteen Jewish and Gentile believing families as part of a core group. To that end, during this period of time the planter will want to be reaching out throughout the community. It might be through Bible studies, having regular Shabbat meals, internet, at holiday meetings and parties, and going door-to-door. We will be reaching out in any number of possible ways to find contacts in the community.

### RECRUITMENT AND COMMUNAL TESTIMONY

Naturally, the planter will be evaluating the people he meets with the idea of congregation planting in mind. A priority with the non-believers he meets is to be sharing the Good News, helping them come to personal faith in Messiah, which he will then be discipling in the faith.

A core group is to be made up of growing disciples, followers of Yeshua. Both Jewish and Gentile believers, which the planter meets may be interested in a Messianic congregation, however their reasons for being a part of a Messianic plant may differ. Each person should be interviewed and evaluated carefully. The interviewer has to find out whether they have already been grounded and rooted in the faith or are new believers. Regardless of their maturity level, a planter will eventually be sharing with them the values and vision of the Messianic congregation he is planting. This is part of the discipleship process, which naturally takes place during core group recruitment and development.

There will be many other people who will not be part of the Messianic congregation, such as people who go to churches throughout the community. It is wrong to seek to recruit people, who are members of other congregations to be part of a new Messianic congregation, as this is sheep stealing. Someone who is already a member of a congregation or a church should be encouraged to grow and bloom where they are planted. On that note, it is also important to be careful of people who are disgruntled. If they are disgruntled with where they currently are they may become just as disgruntled with you as well.

In the cases where you are meeting Christians, you want to let them know you are also a born again believer. This may seem obvious but many Christians misunderstand the Messianic world and they are wary of how different a Messianic congregation is from their church. They may actually think that a group's Messianic Jewish distinctiveness means a difference in primary beliefs

NOTES:

(e.g., on the deity of Messiah and on His gracious work in saving sinners). You will want to emphasize primary beliefs, that you love the Lord, believe God's Word, and that you are "born again" (John 3:3), etc. Though you should not seek their membership in the congregation plant, you should desire their prayers for your work. For some, it is important to understand on a basic level that a Messianic congregation in their area is a genuine part of the body of Messiah.

During this period of time, as the planter is recruiting people for the core group, it is also important to meet local Christian leaders and other leaders throughout the local area. The Spirit of God probably already has other people there who are living for Him and proclaiming the Good News in an area, even if it is an area without Messianic congregations. The planter is probably not the first or the last word on the matter of the Good News. Thus, a wise planter will meet local leaders to share his values and vision. Like others believers, Christian leaders (e.g., pastors) may also misunderstand the Messianic movement. Share with them your values and vision for the work God has put upon your heart. It may be helpful to ask them if they have any questions, and to have a business card to leave with them. You may want to be able to discuss from Romans, etc., the Biblical foundations of a Messianic congregation with them.

You may meet some pastors who might take exception to the work you are doing, or even find it threatening for whatever reason. Availability for such leaders is important, so they may contact you directly if any issues arises. I note this because if they feel threatened by another congregation planted in their area, they may be quick to accept any negative reports about you or your work. Thus, the planter should make himself available to clarify or respond to such matters.

NOTES:

People and groups who are friendly with what you are doing may be interested in sharing space with a Messianic congregation. Many local churches have been quite open to allowing Messianic congregations to utilize the space they have on Saturdays. In such circumstances, this can be a mutual blessing for both the church and the Messianic congregation.

## MATERIAL PREPARATIONS

The Articles of Faith will be the primary teachings (or doctrines), which will distinguish your congregation in light of its faith. A Constitution for the congregation will state its values, by-laws and policies. The congregation is not to be run by the power of the planter's personality but rather by even-handed, fair-minded policies, in which all will be able to understand and abide with.

A Values Statement which will explain the congregation's core values , as well as a Mission Statement, which explains why the congregation exists, will help the core group understand what the congregation is about and what you hope to accomplish. (*See appendix 2 and 3*)

There will need to be a location for meeting, a convenient place for people to get to, as well as equipment for start up. A start-up congregation sometimes has to borrow many items because you may not have the resources or finances to buy the equipment you may want to utilize. Be on the look-out for things you may borrow or utilize for the time being.

Fruit trees take a while to develop roots and produce fruit. Likewise this initial phase will take time, three to six months, or more.

## CORE GROUP DEVELOPMENT

In the Good News accounts we see planters being trained, and in the beginning of Acts is a type of core group development, which takes place (Acts 1-5). With your core group, weekly meetings should primarily function as training sessions. The leader gathers people together for discipling and teaching, getting them grounded and rooted in the basic things, which make up a Messianic congregation. The length of this phase will depend upon how the group has already begun to form during the initial phase or earlier. Until the completion of core group development, the group should not be considered a congregation; the core group is not yet ready to handle the responsibilities of a congregation.

NOTES:

### VISION: UNITY OF VALUES (INSTRUCTION STAGE)

During the first stage, the focus is on instruction in the vision and values of a congregation. A unity of the values has to do with the agreement with the Articles of Faith, the By-Laws, the Values Statement, Mission Statement, and Vision Statement which were developed and collected during the initial phase. You will be reviewing all of these statements in greater detail, along with discussion on culture and the Messianic expression of faith in this congregation.

When we talk about people being *talmidim,* we are referring to followers of Yeshua. The values should not change based on a change in expression. Unity of values is very important in Scripture. It states in Amos 3:3: "How can two walk together lest they are in agreement?" This is true in every Messianic congregation. This unity of values will come because they are unified on the Articles of Faith, the very basic and primary beliefs and is the spiritual fabric uniting the congregation.

In this way your team will be able to distinguish primary from the secondary teachings. On secondary teachings there will be a lot of liberty and varying opinions. However, our unity is in the primary matters of faith. There is no room for disagreement on the primary matters of our faith. This disagreement will only mean division. When you get through the Values portion, there will be teaching on the essential systems of a Messianic congregation.

### BODY: UNITY OF PRIORITIES (INTEGRATION STAGE)

In this stage, the vision and values are fleshed out and integrated into congregational life, as seen in the responsibilities and systems of the congregation. This integration stage may take from two weeks to five months. There should be a focus on outreach, discipleship, and eventually service, which will become part of the DNA of the congregation. Yes, there may be a need for training on evangelism, discipleship, prayer, bible study, and whatever else is expected to be properly functioning in a healthy congregation. The three responsibilities of Prayer, ministry of the Word, and Overseer will be explored in detail during this stage. The primacy of Yeshua as our Head in all these responsibilities is to be stressed.

The core group should understand what primary responsibilities make up a healthy congregation. They need to understand these very responsibilities and as they apply them to their homes, and only then they are able to apply it in the congregation. As they grow in proper leadership in their homes, they will be able to grow into leadership in the community as well.

NOTES:

The functionality of the systems can be related to the core group with respect to the end goals of being self-propagating, self-supporting, and self-governing congregation. These are aspects of a mature congregation and show how each system relates to the next.

A congregation needs as a goal to be self-propagating—doing outreach and winning its community to the Lord. A group must not become in-grown, nor may it expect all of its community to be transferring from other established groups. When "transfer growth" is carried out intentionally, it's considered sheep stealing. Self-propagation is that part of the process of contact making, which leads to disciple making; as a group reaches out to "all with ears to hear" and makes *talmidim* from all nations.

A congregation should also aim to be self-supporting. This is important for mature congregations even if they are a part of a larger congregation planting group which resources them. Revenues and resources for the ministry of the congregation should come from within the body, regardless of socioeconomic conditions. (On that point, however, a good planter will identify with those he is ministering to, and not seek to live a lavishly, just as Yeshua in his incarnation came as one of the ordinary people.) In this respect, it is important that leadership teach tithing of time, talent, and treasure. Self-support is part of what it means for disciples becoming members, by taking responsibility for the expenses of their community; the group matures as they learn to trust the Lord for all they have and put their resources to godly use.

Finally, a maturing congregation should seek to be self-governing. This means there are no outside groups dictating terms, though of course accountability in a congregation's own decisions to the greater Body of Messiah is healthy. Self-governance is part of the goal of members becoming leaders, so that a congregation is empowered from within as the Holy Spirit leads.

### ACTIVITY: UNITY OF SERVICE (APPLICATION STAGE)

Once there is unity of values, and understanding of the systems of a congregation, then there needs to be delegation of tasks relevant to those systems.

Various responsibilities are to be delegated. "What are our responsibilities?" If you were to walk into a congregational service on any Saturday morning as well as activities during the week, what would you expect to see? Maybe you would expect there would be a worship service. This implies the need for a worship team, people who will lead in worship and prayer. A leader may ask, "Why can't I do that?" While a planter must be able and willing to lead in prayer and may even have musical ability, the goal of a Messianic congregation is for members to be eventually leading in the ministry. He and/or his spouse should not attempt to do everything themselves.

What else would you see if you came into a congregation on a Saturday morning? There might be people to greet you if you are a visitor. Likewise, then, you will want to be able to have greeters, people who will welcome the visitors coming in. There are many such tasks, which will be taken on in light of the gifts and calling they have in service for the Lord.

As we consider these crucial areas, you want to take in to account the children. Even if you do not have children, others do. Knowing there is a ministry for their children, people with families will feel at home in your congregation. This might include having a nursery as well.

The leader needs to be delegating these various aspects, including promotion, publicity, and all the various other things, which make up a congregation. You ask, "Where are these people going to come from?" Your core group members. The core group is being developed so they can be involved in the activities

NOTES:

of the congregation. Their participation in the congregation makes it a living example of the body of Messiah, not just an audience for one person's teaching and preaching.

During this stage of core group development you want to see databases and budgets developed. In order for monies to be collected, one should apply to be recognized as a non-profit entity (a 501-C3 in the United States). This is very important to have if you want to give tax-deductible receipts for the tithing and offerings in the congregation. And of course, you will need to set up bank accounts.

You will also need a treasurer. Even if you are supported from outside the congregation (or even if you are independently wealthy), the people of the congregation need to be taught to tithe, donate funds, their time and their talents for their personal maturity and for the growth of the community itself. There is also a need to handle funds properly under the laws of the state.

Another aspect to consider is the design of your materials (such as bulletins and announcements), internet presence (website, social media), and logo. Look for someone with an eye for practicality and good design (and even some training in this area wouldn't hurt), as the internet and all things visual are an increasingly important part of a congregation's identity. This should be understood as part of the contact making system, along with other responsibilities like oneg and the greeters, and all other ministries that are outward in focus. Oneg is a time to meet visitors.

NOTES:

In summary, first come unity of values, then unity of priorities, and finally unity of service as tasks are delegated according to these priorities. While all this is going on, the calendar should be sketched out with the people. Take time to plan for the various festivals and activities, mindful of how these times will become crucial elements in the testimony of the congregation. All who will join you might not share same past experiences, for example, some believers may have never celebrated Passover, while others may have been blessed to grow up with Passover but never understood the joy of Messiah in it. Various materials, such as *haggadot* for Passover, might be needed at those times.

These matters become part of the process of planning towards a consecration service. This will be an evident goal when the core group is ready for initial but functional systems; making sure the children are being taught the Word of God; an outreach is going on; worship is being established, and so on. All of these are early systems, which need to be created during core group development, and to be fully implemented in the establishment phase, which follows.

A consecration service is when the core group is recognized as a congregation. Again, up until that time it is my suggestion that the core-group does not call itself a congregation. Alternatives names include "fellowship," "*havurah*," "Bible study," "*minyan*," etc.

## CONGREGATIONAL DEVELOPMENT

Being a congregation implies having unity of values and priorities, services which are led by committed members, proper delegation of responsibilities for the proper functioning of the essential systems. It more generally implies being a center in the community for worship, instruction, fellowship, and evangelism. The consecration service provides an official milestone in which the congregation itself is birthed.

### Foundation Phase (Leaders in Training)

This phase can be thought of as the birth and early development of the congregation, beginning with the congregation's first service. During this time the essential responsibilities of the congregation should be covered. There will be a need to maintain things well and wisely as excitement builds.

You will want to be inviting various people to this first consecration service. Remember those pastors in the community that you asked to pray for you (or rented you space), I encourage you to ask them to come and to pray for you publicly. You will want to invite other friends of the congregation, which are people that might never become actual members, perhaps, and will always pray for you and stand with the congregation and be friends and visitors on a regular basis. You should also plan on having a nice oneg. Once you have had your consecration service, you are a congregation! At this point in time, if core group development has happened properly, there will already be regular ministry going on.

As regards to types of ministry, there are two kinds of congregations: community congregations and commuter congregations. Most Messianic congregations at this point are commuter congregations, which means that the majority of the people will have to travel, sometimes long distances, to get to a Messianic service. In such congregations the ministry generally has to be "stacked" on Shabbat, since people might not be able to meet as often during the work week. However, as community develops in proximity to the congregation, there may be opportunities to develop more activities throughout the week. There should be a strong focus on training classes in Scripture and Messianic life, as well as a focus on ministering to children.

NOTES:

# Congregational Development Schedule

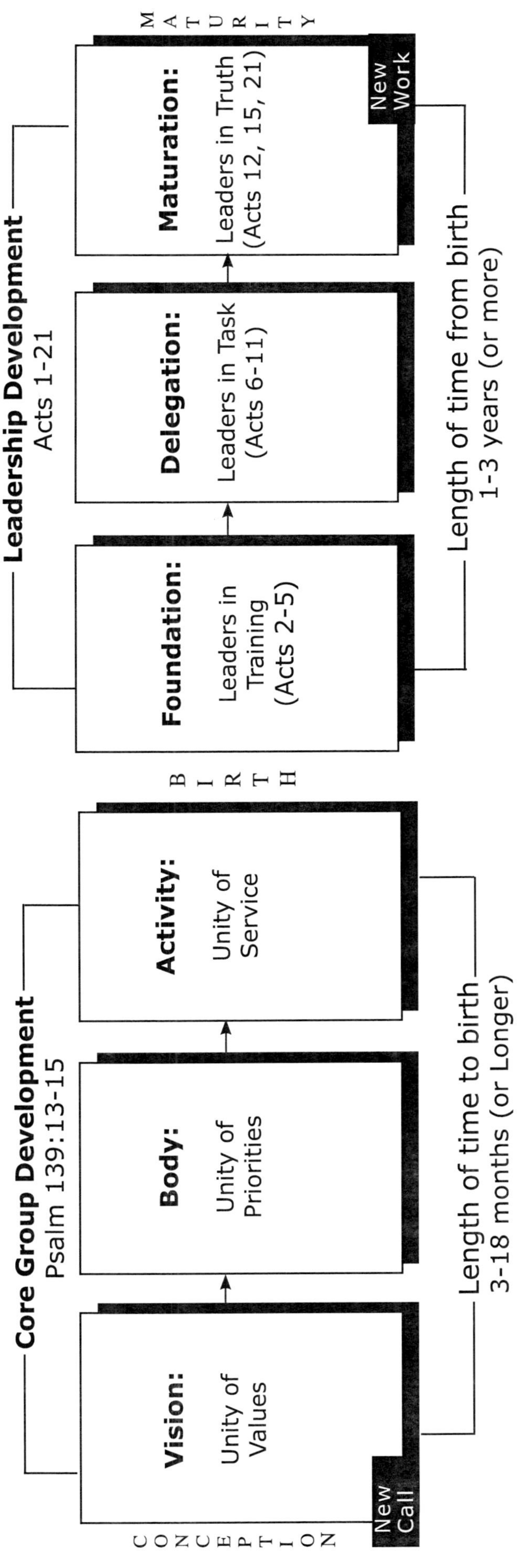


*Figure 3.2*

### Delegation stage (leaders in task)

One can think of this as a time of adolescence for the congregation. In the Scriptures during this stage (Acts 6-11), not only administration of feeding widows but even personal suffering was delegated, as Stephen was martyred for the testimony of Yeshua. During this time Barnabas and others were also raised up and delegated responsibility in the early Messianic community.

In the congregation this is a time of intense development, where those who have gone through leadership training are now being developed as leaders through personal experience. By this stage, more people than the planter and his original partners are able to make judgment calls about areas of service in the congregation. Leaders have been developed as such that they have responsibility, authority, and accountability. Responsibility clearly explains the charge; authority refers to the resources to accomplish the charge; and accountability denotes the obligation to properly accomplish the charge.

The development of the congregation in this stage is seen as maturing as it has responsible, empowered, and accountable leaders. The leadership is developing people who lead in prayer, teach, preach, coordinate ministries, manage the work of the congregation, and start new initiatives in the congregation.

### Maturation stage (leaders in truth)

Just as a young person is meant to grow to maturity and even reproduce, we can think of this stage as a reproduction stage in that it can result in a new work. In Acts 12:17 and reiterated in Acts 15:22-23, we see how local leadership ("the elders") were entrusted with leading the congregation at Jerusalem, and the Apostles and others were enabled to start new congregations throughout the region.

There should come a time when the planter is no longer needed for the congregation to continue, however he might be asked to continue to serve with the congregation as an elder or rabbi. The goal is accomplished, the congregation is now self-propagating, self-supporting, and self-governing. This mature congregation is ready to reproduce, that is, start new congregations in new areas, and as such the cycle begins again.

# APPENDICES

# SUPPLEMENTAL MATERIAL

Appendix 1

# Messianic Congregations and the Greater Body of Messiah

In order to live for the glory of God, the ultimate goal of a Messianic congregation is not merely to effectively communicate Messiah to the Jewish people, but to stimulate the body of Yeshua to love and good works, especially as it pertains to the Jewish people. These five steps address a Messianic congregation's approach to the body of Messiah.

## I. Identification with the Body (Ephesians 4:4-6)

Messianic communities are a part of the body. Though established as self-supported, self-governed, and self-propagating, a congregation's Articles of Faith should evidence identification with faith in Yeshua as understood in evangelical and orthodox circles. There is only one Body of Messiah made up Jewish and Gentile followers of Yeshua. Therefore, this Body agrees on the primary teachings of the faith once delivered.

Not all who go by the name "Messianic" (or "Christian") are truly part of the Body, but may have deviated from the faith. The primary teachings regarding the nature of God (e.g. Triune), the nature of man, Messiah's work, Salvation by faith in what Yeshua has done, the authority of Scriptures help clarify that which unifies a Messianic congregation with the greater Body. Furthermore, within the congregation there must be a recognition equality between Jews and Gentiles, whether in evangelism (needing the Gospel), discipleship (needing to grow), membership (needing to serve), and leadership (called to care).

*What this necessitates from the congregation:* An attitude of affirmation of the Body, stripped of anti-church attitudes (let alone anti-Gentile mindsets) (Eph 4:1-3, 29). We are to love the whole Body of Messiah, and denounce any sinful attitudes which are both improper for any believer and contrary to our calling as a Messianic congregation. However, a congregation should not have fellowship with those who curse Israel or speak against its establishment (Genesis 12:3, Number 24:9; Rom 9:3). These are in error and we will seek to restore them to fellowship (Gal 6:1).

## II. COMMUNICATION TO THE BODY (ROMANS 12:3-6)

Messianic congregations should present themselves to the larger body of Messiah as a part which is most able to communicate corporately, culturally, and biblically to the Jewish community that Yeshua is the Messiah, as well as to the larger Body that God has not forsaken the Jewish people. Specifically, the whole Body of believers in the area should see the local Messianic congregation as partners in their own testimony to the Jewish community, representing the truth that Yeshua is both the Savior of all who believe and believing in Him does not lessen one's Jewish identity (John 3:36; 8:24, etc).

*What this necessitates from the congregation:* An active outreach to the Body of Messiah: whether through website promotion, newsletters, speaking at church meetings, Bible studies, conferences, or just relationship building over lunch.

## III. ACCESSIBILITY FOR THE BODY (1 CORINTHIANS 14:16-17)

Messianic congregations can provide opportunity for the whole body of Messiah in their area to have Jewish acquaintances come and hear the message of Messiah. In fact, even in a Messianic congregation, services should be friendly enough for all visitors, in order for the message of the Messiah to be understood by all people (1 Corinthians 2:1-5, etc).

*What this necessitates from the congregation:* continue to strive to be visitor-friendly with materials and outreach to them. Through promotion, holiday and special services can be made accessible for local churches in light of their Jewish friends and neighbors: "Invite a Jewish friend to Passover (Purim, Shabbat)!"

## IV. Service in the Body (1 Corinthians 9:19-23)

Messianic congregations can provide training for the larger Body of Messiah so that churches themselves will be able to share the message of Messiah in a way that Jewish people can understand, as well as disciple Jewish people to be an ongoing witness of the Jewish Messiah in the Jewish community and in the general Body.

Congregations recognize two realities. First, the majority of Jewish people who come to faith do so through sincere believers and churches, not Messianic congregations. Second, of the many Jews in churches around the country, few are discipled to remain Jewish or raise their children as Jewish.

Classes should be open to members and non-members alike and some classes designed to help all people learn how to be an effective witness to the Jewish people. Also, integrity insists there must be Messianic training on discipleship and how to evangelize, so people will grow as they are won.

*What this necessitates from the congregation:* Area-wide Promotion of all classes and message series. This may include Jewish evangelism and other specific training made available to the whole body, providing materials for both evangelism and discipleship. Teachers and worship leaders can also be equipped to go to local churches for Sunday school classes and mid-week meetings. Many members should be able to teach on Romans 11, the Feasts of Israel, and the Jewish context of the New Covenant.

NOTES:

## V. Encouragement for the Body (Romans 11:11)

We are called to minister and not manipulate. Ministry is encouraging people in what they know they need to be doing. Manipulation is encouraging people to do what you want them to be doing.

Many evangelical churches in the area want to grow in their witness of Messiah to the local and worldwide Jewish community. In this regard, they need to be encouraged to fulfill the mutual and biblical call between Jewish and Gentile believers with equal partnership in Messiah's Great Commission (Rom 1:16; 11:11, etc). The larger body of Messiah will more effectively communicate to the Jewish people as the body understands the faithfulness of God's character pertaining to both the Jewish people and the nations. Consequently, they will use their liberty in Messiah as regards to behavior and congregational life in order to more effectively testify to the Jewish people and all people what the God of Israel has accomplished through salvation in Yeshua.

*What this necessitates from the congregation:* development of materials on this calling upon the whole Body of Messiah (see Messianic Foundations); seeking opportunities to teach series on these matters within churches (Sunday school classes, etc.): planning provided for effective Jewish ministry in and with those churches; and development of partnership forums for outreach programs and training.

The following illustration shows us how we to reflect the culture of heaven when it comes to care for one another: There was once a man who had a nightmare about hell. He saw an abundance of wonderful food everywhere. The problem was that the people had to eat with six foot chopsticks! People could not get the food to their mouths. Then he had a dream about heaven. There was the same situation: wonderful food, and six foot chopsticks! Why then was it heaven? Because in heaven, people were feeding one another! Getting our own food and looking out for ourselves is not the goal, but rather feeding one another.

Our care for one another testifies of God's program of restoration on earth. The commonwealth of Israel (the whole Body) is meant to reveal the King of Israel's love for the people of Israel. And Jewish believers have a calling to the whole Body of Messiah.

Appendix 2

# Sample Constitution Including Covenant, By-Laws, and Articles of Faith

## Covenant

Having been led, as we believe, by the Spirit of God to receive the Messiah Yeshua as our Savior and Lord, and on the profession of our faith having been immersed in the name of the Father, and of the Son, and of the Holy Spirit, we do now, in the presence of God, angels and this assembly, most joyfully enter into Covenant with one another, as one body in Messiah.

We agree, therefore, to be led by the Holy Spirit:

- ✡ To walk together in Messiah's love;
- ✡ To knit together Jew and Gentile in one local fellowship to worship the God of Israel;
- ✡ To reach out to the community with the love of God found in the promised Messiah of Israel;
- ✡ To be supportive of the State of Israel as exhorted in the Holy Scriptures and pray for the peace of Jerusalem;
- ✡ To strive for the advancement of this congregation in wisdom, holiness, and love;

- ✡ To promote its prosperity and spiritual growth;
- ✡ To sustain its worship, ordinances, discipline, and doctrine;
- ✡ To give it a sacred preeminence over all institutions of human origin;
- ✡ To contribute cheerfully and regularly to the support of the ministry, the expenses of the congregation, the relief of the poor, and the spread of the gospel through all nations;

We also agree:

- ✡ To maintain family and personal devotions;
- ✡ To faithfully educate our children in the Word of God;
- ✡ To seek the salvation of our kindred and acquaintances;
- ✡ To walk circumspectly in the world;
- ✡ To be just in our dealings, faithful in our engagements, and exemplary in our deportment;
- ✡ To avoid all gossiping and inappropriate anger;
- ✡ To abstain from all forms of evil;
- ✡ To be prepared for the defense of the Good News;
- ✡ To extend love in removing all prejudices, especially anti-Semitism;
- ✡ To be zealous in our efforts to advance the kingdom of our Messiah;

We further agree:

- ✡ To watch over one another in brotherly love;
- ✡ To pray for one another;
- ✡ To aid each other in sickness and distress;
- ✡ To cultivate sympathy in feeling and courtesy in speech;
- ✡ To be slow to take offense, to be always ready for reconciliation and mindful of the restoration of our Messiah to secure it without delay.
- ✡ "To further clarify (but not delimit) the meaning of the above-stated covenant "[t]o abstain from all forms of evil", we agree that the term "marriage" has only one meaning, to wit, marriage sanctioned by God which joins one man and one woman in a single, exclusive union, as

delineated in the Bible; that God intends sexual activity to occur only between a man and a woman who are married to each other; that God has forbidden sexual activity outside of a marriage between a man and a woman; and that any form of sexual immorality or sexual activity outside of a marriage between a man and a woman, including without limitation, cross-dressing, promiscuity, adultery, fornication, homosexuality, bisexual conduct, transsexual conduct, polyamorous conduct, bestiality, incest, pedophilia, pornography or any attempt to change one's gender, or disagreement with one's biological gender, is evil, sinful and offensive to God.

We also agree that in order to preserve the function and integrity of the congregation as the local Body of Messiah, and to provide a Biblically accurate witness to the congregation members and to the surrounding community, it is imperative that all members of the congregation and persons employed by the congregation, including without limitation volunteers who are in a position of responsibility and authority over children and those employed as congregational staff, agree to and abide by the foregoing statement on marriage and sexuality and conduct themselves accordingly."

We moreover agree, that when we remove from this place, we will as soon as possible unite with some other congregation of like faith and practice, where we can carry out the spirit of this covenant and the principles of God's Word.

NOTES:

## CONSTITUTION: BY LAWS

### ARTICLE I - NAME

The name of the congregation shall be [inserr name]. The principal office of the congregation shall be located at [insert address]

### ARTICLE II - PURPOSE

Our purpose is to maintain an indigenous, autonomous congregation under God; to promote the spirit of the early New Covenant congregation in the spreading of the Good News of Messiah Yeshua; to knit together Jew and Gentile in one local fellowship to worship the God of Israel; to maintain a testimony of the truth of the Good News and purity of the congregation (Matthew 28:18-20, I Corinthians 15:1-4); also to encourage our congregation planters at home and abroad, and to help them in their needs; to be supportive of the state of Israel as exhorted in the Holy Scriptures (Psalm 122:6).

We want to maintain a standard of Biblical separation from worldliness and apostasy; and to actively, positively and assertively live for the faith, which was once delivered to the believers in Yeshua (Jude 3).

The congregation, in recognizing its unique calling to reach out to all people, but especially to the Jew first (Romans 1:16), will have at its services a Jewish identity in worship; not to offend any Gentile brethren, but in order to reflect to the community the congregation's sensitivities and understanding of the Scriptures regarding Israel's Messiah who is the Savior of the world and to demonstrate as a congregation that God in Messiah has not forsaken His people Israel. The congregation, made up of Jew and Gentile alike, further understands that this testimony will always be secondary to the testimony of their love one for another to the Glory of God.

## ARTICLE III - MEMBERSHIP

SECTION I - RECEPTION: Any person applying for membership with this congregation shall be examined and recommended by the Membership Committee consisting of the Z'keinim, Congregation Leader, and other members approved by the Board of Z'keinim. Such person shall have first attended the congregation for at least four Shabbat services, give evidence of their salvation by personal testimony, shall have been immersed, be willing to serve in the congregation, and shall agree to uphold the Covenant of this congregation.

In furtherance of the foregoing, all such persons shall believe in Messiah Yeshua as Savior and Lord; shall actively pursue and continue in a vital fellowship with Messiah Yeshua in thought, word and deed; shall affirm all tenets of the Consideration of Values, Covenant, By-Laws and Articles of Faith; and shall offer evidence, by their confession and their conduct, that they are living in accord with their vital fellowship with Messiah Yeshua and with their affirmation of the tenets of the Consideration of Values, Covenant, By-Laws and Articles of Faith. Such persons shall attend membership classes and fulfill any prerequisites the Membership Committee deems necessary. Such applicants thus recommended shall be voted upon by the congregation and must receive a two-thirds majority of the votes cast.

This congregation will welcome into its membership by letter, any person giving evidence of salvation by a personal testimony and upon receipt of a letter of recommendation from any congregation maintaining the same or similar doctrinal stand. Recommendation by the committee will be made upon receipt of the letter and after investigation of the sending congregation. These will then be voted upon by the congregation and must receive a two-thirds majority of the votes cast.

NOTES:

## SECTION II - CLASSIFICATION

- Active - A member shall be considered active if he regularly attends the services, gives evidence of his support of the Articles of Faith, is not under discipline, and has not been dismissed from membership.
- Inactive - After appropriate inquiry or examination by the Board of Z'keinim, a member shall be considered inactive if he does not regularly attend worship services (except if he is unable) or is under discipline. An inactive member shall forfeit the privileges of membership. Inactive members are to be advised in writing by the Board of Z'keinim. To be reinstated as an active member, an inactive member must follow the procedures for the reception of new members.
- Non-Participating Members - Members that are by necessity of circumstances not in the general area of the congregation for an extended period of time, will be able to maintain their membership. However they will be considered "non participating members" and will not be considered for quorum and will not have a vote.

## SECTION III - RESPONSIBILITIES AND PRIVILEGES OF MEMBERS

Responsibilities:

- It shall be the responsibility of every member to attend all regular meetings and to manifest a keen interest in the up-building of the congregation.
- It shall be the responsibility of every member to practice stewardship of both talents and substance for the well being of the congregation. Every member, depending on their circumstances, is expected to be active in congregational service and tithing.
- It shall be the responsibility of every member to guard the testimony of the congregation and its leadership before non-members and each other by a spoken and unyielding loyalty to fellow members as an example of close fellowship with our Messiah Yeshua.

Privileges:

- It shall be the privilege of every active member 18 years of age and over to vote in the affairs of the congregation. All members between the ages of 13 and 17 may apply to the Board of Z'keinim for the privilege to vote.
- It shall be the privilege of every active member to hold office and serve on committees and boards.

NOTES:

- ✡ It shall be the privilege of every active member to use the facilities of the congregation for weddings, funerals, Bar/Bat Mitzvah and other related affairs upon approval by the Board of Shamashim/Deacons or Z'keinim.
- ✡ It shall be the privilege of every active member to receive all routine congregational communications, newsletters, etc.
- ✡ It shall be the privilege of every active member to receive advice and counsel from the Pastoral leadership of the congregation or its delegates.
- ✡ It shall be the privilege of all active members, to have their children dedicated to the Lord at a congregational service.
- ✡ It shall be the privilege of all active members to have the pastoral staff perform their wedding ceremonies following the required premarital counseling and agreement by the officiant.

## SECTION IV - DISMISSAL

- ✡ By Letter - Any member who wishes to unite with another congregation of like faith may, upon request of that congregation, be granted a letter of recommendation dependent on the approval by the Board of Z'keinim.
- ✡ By Erasure - Any member whose residence has been unknown to the congregation for one year or who has failed to attend for one year shall have his name erased from the roll. This will be done upon recommendation of the Board of Z'keinim and after sending a registered letter to his last known address. The congregation will then vote upon the erasure; a two-thirds majority of votes cast will complete the erasure at the congregational business meeting.
- ✡ By Removal - A friend of the congregation's (FOC) name is removed upon approval of the Board of Z'keinim when he ceases to regularly attend the services.
- ✡ By Death - The death of a member automatically dissolves membership
- ✡ By Expulsion - When the congregation, in the exercise of its constitutional authority in discipline, withdraws fellowship from one proven to be an unworthy member, his membership immediately ceases. This shall be done only after enjoining scriptural steps and in light of Galatians 6:1, Matthew 18:15-20, and I Corinthians 5:9-13.
- ✡ By Request - Any person requesting that his name be removed can be so removed by personal notification. The congregation may not accept

NOTES:

the resignation from any member charged with conduct unbecoming a member or who is currently under congregational discipline until those charges have been investigated and that member cleared or the matter has been resolved.

## ARTICLE IV - OFFICES AND ELECTION

***A) Board of Trustees*** - The Board of Trustees shall consist of a minimum of three (3) trustees made up of Congregation Leaders, Z'keinim, Shamashim, and those deemed responsible by the Board of Trustees. Trustees may serve maximum of two three (3) year terms before stepping down for at least one year.

Members of the Board of Trustees shall be active members of the congregation. New members of the Board of Trustees will be presented by the Board of Z'keinim to be voted on by majority vote of members present.

The extent of terms of membership of the Board of Trustees will be three (3), two (2), and one (1) year terms for the first slate of Trustees.

The trustees will be responsible for the fiscal affairs of the congregation under the oversight of the Board of Z'keinim. They will prepare a yearly budget that will reflect ministry priorities of the Z'keinim that will be approved by two-thirds majority of the congregation at the yearly business meeting. They will also provide a quarterly financial report comparing actual giving and expenditures to the budget.

NOTES:

The Congregation shall have the following Officers who shall be elected in the manner described below:

***President*** – The Congregational Leader shall serve as President and shall be chosen in the manner set forth in Article IV (B) below.

The following officers shall be elected by the Board of Z'keinim (Elders): Secretary & Treasurer.

The Board of Z'keinim may elect such other Officers including one or more Vice-Presidents, one or more Assistant Secretaries, and one or more Assistant Treasurers, as seems desirable, such Officers to have the authority and perform the duties prescribed from time to time, by the Board of Z'keinim. The following rules shall govern the term and duties of the Officers:

*a. Election and Term of Office.* The Officers shall be elected for terms of one year beginning on January 1 of each year and shall be elected by the Board of Z'keinim (except for the President - Congregational Leader, who shall be elected as set forth in Subparagraph (B) below) in December of each year to serve for the following year. The Board of Z'keinim shall promptly fill any vacancies in the corporate offices. Vacancies in any office shall be promptly filled.

*b. President.* The President (Congregational Leader) shall be authorized to execute all documents and take all action which are required to be done by the President under the laws of the State of North Carolina. The President shall also have the duties of the congregational Leader as set forth herein.

*c. Secretary.* The Secretary shall keep the minutes of the meetings of the members and the Board of Trustees in one or more books provided for that purpose; see that all notices are duly given in accordance with the provisions of these By Laws or as required by law; be custodian of the records and see that the Seal of the Corporation is affixed to all documents, the execution of which on behalf of the Congregation under seal is authorized in accordance with the provisions of these By Laws; keep a register of the post office address of each member which shall be furnished to the Secretary by each member; and in general perform all duties instant to the office of Secretary and such other duties as from time to time may be assigned by the Board of Trustees.

*d. Treasurer.* The Treasurer shall: 1) Have charge and custody of and be responsible for all funds and securities of the Congregation; keep and maintain adequate and correct accounts of the Congregation's properties and business transactions; bring reports and accounting to the leadership and members; receive and give receipts for money due and payable to the Congregation from any source whatsoever, and deposit all monies in the name of the Congregation, in such banks, trust companies or such other depositories as shall be selected by the Board of Trustees; 2) In general, perform all the duties instant to the office of Treasurer and such other duties as from time to time may be assigned by the *Board of Trustees.*

***B) Congregational Leader*** - the Congregational Leader will be a voting member of the Board of Z'keinim and will be responsible for the spiritual growth and welfare of the congregation. The Congregation Leader, a servant of God, must be in accord with the Constitution. In order to become Congregation Leader, he must be examined by the Board of Z'keinim and voted on by the congregation for a four-fifths majority of the votes cast at a congregational meeting for the calling of the Congregation Leader.

The Congregation Leader shall serve until his leadership is terminated by resignation or by request of the Board of Z'keinim and the congregation. If at any time the Congregation Leader's personal belief, preaching or conduct shall not be in full accord with the Constitution of the congregation, his services as Congregation Leader may be terminated by a two-thirds majority of the votes cast at any duly called congregational meeting. Congregational meetings, where the subject is the dismissal of the Congregation Leader, must be announced two weeks prior to the meeting date(s). The resignation of the Congregation Leader must be given to the Board of Z'keinim and congregation at least one (1) month prior to his departure. Upon removal or resignation of the Congregation Leader, the Z'keinim will move to establish a Congregation

NOTES:

Leader search committee made up of Z'keinim, Shamashim-Shamashot, and other members of the congregation. The Congregation Leader at any annual meeting may call a confidence vote.

***C) Board of Z'keinim*** - The Board of Z'keinim will be the men responsible for the spiritual oversight of the congregation. Z'keinim will be selected by the Board of Z'keinim and affirmed by a two-thirds majority of votes cast at a congregational meeting. If a Zakkein is found to be spiritually unfit, a two-thirds majority of votes cast at a congregational meeting will dismiss him from the Board of Z'keinim. The extent of terms of membership of the Board of Z'keinim will be three (3), two (2), and one (1) year terms for the first slate of Z'keinim. Z'keinim, with the exception of the Congregation Leader, may serve maximum of two three (3) year terms before stepping down for at least one year.

Z'keinim will be responsible for the oversight of the Worship, Teaching, Outreach, and Administration of the congregation whether it is through visitation, discipleship, congregational discipline, Shabbat school, Chavurot, evangelism, congregational Web Pages, etc. The work of ministry will be accomplished by them generally through the delegation of those duties to other responsible members of the congregation.

Any account involving a member who is accused of violating the Consideration of Values, Covenant, By-Laws and/or Articles of Faith shall be directed to the Board of Z'keinim to be handled according to Scripture Matthew 5:23-24, 18:15-18, Galatians 6:1. In furtherance of the foregoing, all final decisions by the Board of Z'keinim regarding the interpretation and application of the Bible on a case-by-case basis, including without limitation such decisions pertaining to the morality, conduct and discipline of congregation members, will be accepted as final by the congregation.

NOTES:

***D) Board of Shamashim*** - The Board of Shamashim will be the men responsible for the operational functioning of the congregation. The Board of Z'keinim will establish the Board of Shamashim. Shamashim will be selected in accordance with biblical standards (I Timothy 3, Acts 6). One becomes a member of the Board of Shamashim by being presented to the congregation by the Board of Z'keinim and affirmed by a two-thirds majority of votes cast at a congregational meeting. The extent of the term for membership of the Board of Shamashim will be two (2) years.

***E) Board of Shamashot/Deaconesses*** - The Board of Shamashot will be the women responsible for helping Z'keinim with counseling, teaching, discipleship, and the operational functions of the congregation. The Board of Z'keinim will establish the Board of Shamashot. Shamashot will be selected in accordance with biblical standards (I Timothy 3). One becomes a member of the Board of Shamashot by being presented to the congregation by the Board of Z'keinim and affirmed by a two-thirds majority of votes cast at a congregational meeting. The extent of term for membership of the Board of Shamashot will be two (2) years.

***F) Shabbat School Superintendent*** - The Shabbat School Superintendent shall be selected by Disciple making Z'keinim or Shamashim/Shamashot and approved by the Board of Z'keinim and by a majority of votes cast at a special congregational meeting. The term shall be two (2) years.

***G) Missions Chairperson*** - the chairperson of the missions committee shall be selected by the Contact-making Z'keinim or Shamashim / Shamashot and approved by the Board of Z'keinim and by majority of votes cast at the annual business meeting. The term shall be for two (2) years.

## ARTICLE V - ORDINATION AND LICENSING

Ordination: When, in the judgment of the Board of Z'keinim, a man in this fellowship has been called of God to minister in the capacity of a pastor, evangelist, or missionary, it shall be the duty of the Board of Z'keinim to determine if the man is faithfully fulfilling the obligation of such a call and is worthy of ordination. It shall then recommend to the congregation the calling of a council to examine the candidate to be invited for said council and the congregational secretary shall send the invitation to each person of the council so invited. The council shall thoroughly examine the candidate as to:

- His salvation experience.
- His call to the ministry.
- His view of Scriptural doctrine.

After which the council will deliberate and decide whether or not to recommend to the congregation his ordination. Upon recommendation of the council, the congregation will vote to affirm the ordination at the congregational meeting.

Licensing: Upon the recommendation of the Congregation Leader, the Board of Z'keinim may also present to the congregation any member of the congregation entering into full-time service and doing the required work of ministry for Messiah.

## ARTICLE VI - CONGREGATIONAL MEETINGS

The annual congregational meeting shall be held the second Shabbat after Sukkot, unless a change is publicly announced on two previous Shabbats and a different date presented no more than one month from the original date. A special congregational meeting may be called by the Congregation Leader, the Board of Z'keinim, or upon the written request of seven (7) members of the congregation to the Board of Z'keinim, and must be announced by the Board of Z'keinim two (2) Shabbats before it is to occur.

NOTES:

Meetings to carry on routine business, such as voting on persons for membership, can be handled at any regular service of the congregation by a majority of voting members present. All duly called meetings are required to have been announced for two (2) previous weeks at regular services and need to have a quorum of one-third (1/3) of participating voting membership of the congregation.

### ARTICLE VII - AMENDMENTS

This constitution may be changed or amended at any annual congregational meeting by a two-thirds (2/3) majority vote of ballots cast.

### ARTICLE VIII - FISCAL YEAR

The fiscal year of the Congregation shall begin on the first day of January and end on the last day of December of in each year.

### ARTICLE IX - CORPORATE SEAL

The Board of Trustee shall provide a Corporate Seal, which shall be in the form of a circle and it shall have inscribed thereon the name of the congregation and the words "Corporate Seal."

### ARTICLE X - FUNDS

No part of the net earnings of the corporation shall inure to the benefit of, its members, directors, officers, or other persons except that the organization shall be authorized and empowered to pay reasonable compensation for services rendered and to make payments and distributions in furtherance of the exempt purposes of the corporation.

In the event of dissolution, the residual assets of the corporation will be turned over to one or more corporations with similar purposes which are exempt as corporations described in Section 501(c ) (3) of the Internal Revenue Code of 1986.

NOTES:

## CONSTITUTION: ARTICLES OF FAITH

***1. We believe*** there is one God, eternally existent in three persons - Father, Son and Holy Spirit. We believe that God is all knowing, all-powerful, ever present, and changeless and that He is holy, righteous, faithful, merciful and loving (Deuteronomy 6:4; Isaiah 43:10-11; 48:16).

***a. We believe*** that the Father is all fullness of the Godhead invisible. We rejoice that He concerns Himself mercifully in the affairs of men, that He hears and answers prayer, and that He saves from sin and death all that come to Him through faith in Messiah Yeshua (Exodus 4:22; Matthew 3:17; John 1:12, 3:16; 8:24, 58; Galatians 3:26).

***b. We believe*** that Messiah Yeshua is the eternal and only begotten Son of God, conceived of the Holy Spirit, born of a Jewish virgin, Miriam. He was sinless in His life and He made atonement for the sins of the world by the shedding of His blood unto death. We believe in His bodily resurrection from the dead, His ascension, His high priestly work in Heaven for us, and His visible pre-millennial return to the world according to His promise. (Leviticus 17:11; Psalm 22:16; 110:4; Isaiah 52:13-53:12; Daniel 9:26; Zechariah 12:10; Mark 10:45; Romans 3:24-26, 5:8-9; 2 Corinthians 5:14, 21; 1 Peter 3:18; Isaiah 7:14, 9:6-7; Jeremiah 23:5-6; Micah 5:2; John 1:1, 8:58; 1 Timothy 3:16; Hebrews 1:2-3; 1 Corinthians 15:3-8; Hebrews 7:1-25, 8;1; 1 John 2:1).

***c. We believe*** the *Ruach HaKodesh* (Holy Spirit) is a person of the Godhead; and as such, He possesses all the distinct attributes of Deity. He is ever present to glorify and testify of Messiah Yeshua. We believe that according to the *Brit Chadashah* (New Covenant), the *Ruach HaKodesh* permanently indwells regenerates, and seals the believer. He empowers, sovereignly imparting at least one spiritual gift to every believer for the purpose of edifying and equipping the Body of Messiah, guides, teaches, sanctifies, and fills believers, convicts the world of sin, righteousness, and judgment.

We believe the immersion of the *Ruach HaKodesh* is both initiatory and universal. Believers should therefore seek to identify, utilize and develop their God given gifts for service in the Lord (Genesis 1:2; Psalm 139:7-8; Nehemiah 9:20; 1 John 5:6; John 14:16-17, 15:26-27, 16:7-15; 1 Corinthians 2:10-11, 12:4-31; 2 Corinthians 13:14; Ephesians 1:13-14, 4:30).

***2. We believe t***hat the Bible is God's completed Word, that it was inerrantly written by divinely inspired men, that it is the supreme, infallible authority in all matters of faith and conduct, and that it is true in all that it affirms (Proverbs 30:5-6; Isaiah 40:7-8; Jeremiah 31:31; Matthew 5:18; 2 Timothy 3:16; 2 Peter 1:21).

***3. We believe*** that humanity was created in the image of God. We believe that because of the original sin that all men are by nature and choice sinful and alienated from God. Man has no possible means of reconciling himself to God and that, by persisting in the sinful state of unbelief, man is justly condemned by God to eternal punishment. (Genesis 1:26-27, 2:17, 3:6; Isaiah 53:6, 64:6; Jeremiah 17:9; Mark 7:20-23; John 2:24-25; Romans 5:12-15; Ephesians 2:1-3).

***4. We believe*** that man is reconciled to God, being justified by grace through faith in the atoning work of Messiah Yeshua. Being reconciled, man has peace with God and direct access to Him through Messiah Yeshua and has the hope of eternal glory in Heaven with God. Further, there is no way of salvation apart from faith in Messiah Yeshua for any person, Jewish or Gentile (Genesis 15:6; Habakkuk 2:4; John 1:12-13; 14:6; Acts 4:12; Romans 3:28; Ephesians 1:7; 1 Timothy 2:5: Titus 3:5).

NOTES:

We believe that all who have truly trusted in Messiah Yeshua are kept eternally secure by the power of God through the new birth, the indwelling and sealing ministry of the Holy Spirit, and the intercession of Messiah Yeshua (John 10:28-30, 14:16-17; Romans 8:38-39; Ephesians 4:30; 1 John 2:1; 1Peter 1:23).

We believe that all who have trusted in Messiah Yeshua, though forgiven, still have to contend with the power of sin in this life. Each believer has the ability to choose sin or righteousness. God has made full provision for believers to live in obedience to Him through the complete atonement of Messiah Yeshua and the indwelling of the Spirit of God (John 17:17-19; Romans 6:1-11, 7:15-25, 8:11-13; 1 John 1:8-2:2).

***5. We believe*** the Congregation is a living, spiritual body of which Messiah Yeshua is the head and all true believers are members. The body of Messiah Yeshua began at *Shavuot* (Pentecost) when believers were filled with the Holy Spirit after the ascension of Messiah Yeshua. It will be completed when the Messiah returns for His bride. The body of Messiah is distinct from Israel and is composed of both Jewish and non-Jewish (Gentile) believers made into one new man by faith in Messiah Yeshua (Matthew 16:18; Acts 1:5, 2:14-38; 1 Corinthians 12:13; Ephesians 2:11-15, 5:23-27; Colossians 1:18-20, 3:14-15).

We believe that the local congregation is an organized body of believers in Messiah Yeshua who have been through *Mikvah / T'avilah* (baptism) by immersion upon confession of faith and who associate for worship, fellowship, teaching, and service. We believe the local congregation is governed by its members through the Z'keinim (Elders) and is not ruled by any outside political authority. Its purpose is to glorify God through worship, instruction, accountability, discipline, fellowship and outreach (Matthew 28:19-20; Acts 2:42-47; Ephesians 4:11-13; Hebrews 10:19-25). We believe Messiah Yeshua commands Zicharon (the Lord's Supper) and believer's Mikvah / T'avilah (baptism) by immersion for observation by the Congregation (Matthew 28:18-20; Luke 22:19-20; 1 Cor. 11:23-26).

***6. We believe*** that Satan is the chief enemy of God and our souls, and that while he continues to rule this present world, Messiah Yeshua's atoning death and resurrection have defeated him. Satan will suffer eternal punishment by being cast into the lake of fire after the Messiah's one thousand year Messianic reign (2 Corinthians 4:4; Ephesians 2:1-3; Colossians 2:15; Revelation 20:10). Satan is the father of lies and anti-Semitism and hostility toward Israel. Believers can and should resist him and his demons by faith, applying Spiritual truth. We believe that though believers cannot be demon possessed, they can be demon oppressed (Genesis 3:1-19; Luke 10:18; John 8:44; Ephesians 6:10-19; James 4:7-8; 1 Peter 5:8-9; Revelation 12:13).

We believe in the God ordained ministry of holy angels to bring about God's intended plans and purposes and to minister to all believers (Isaiah 6:1-7; Daniel 10:10-21; Luke 15:10; Ephesians 1:21; Hebrews 1:14; Revelation 7:11-12).

NOTES:

*7. **We believe*** the people of Israel, comprised of the physical descendants of Abraham, Isaac, and Jacob, and are chosen by God. The Abrahamic Covenant expressed God's choice of Israel and His irrevocable, unconditional covenant to the Jewish people. Jewish believers have a unique two-fold identity as both the spiritual remnant of physical Israel and as members of the body of Messiah Yeshua. Non-Jewish believers become adopted sons and daughters of Abraham and partakers of the spiritual blessings of Israel and are therefore grafted into the Jewish Olive Tree for service.

We believe that it is the believer's duty and privilege to communicate the Good News of Messiah Yeshua to the Jewish people first, and also to the Gentiles, according to the Scriptures, in a clear yet sensitive way. It is also the believer's duty to support the God given rights of Israel to the land while opposing anti-Semitism according to the provisions of the Abrahamic Covenant. We believe God has a special purpose and role for the nation of Israel and the Jewish people. We believe in the full physical and spiritual restoration of Israel at the Second Coming of the Messiah as proclaimed in the Scriptures (Genesis 12:1-3; 17:7-8, 26:3-4, 28:13-15; Exodus 19:6; Amos 3:2; 9:8; Zechariah 12:10; 14:2-4; Matthew 23:39; John 4:22; Acts 3:19-21, 13:46; Romans 1:16, 9:3-5; 10:1-5; 11:2-5, 23-26, 28-29; Ephesians 2:14-19).

The Law is not, nor was it ever, a means of justification or sanctification, which come by grace through faith alone. Believers in Yeshua are under the New Covenant, which is not like the Mosaic covenant, and which the law of Moses eagerly awaited. However, both Jewish and non-Jewish believers have a stewardship to utilize the law of Moses as it is applied through New Covenant revelation. For non-Jewish believers as well as Jewish believers, observances such as the festivals and Shabbat are a means of expressing the faithfulness of God to His people (Deuteronomy 29:1--34:10; Jeremiah 31:31-33; Acts 21:24-25; Romans 6:14-15; 8:2-9; 10:4-9; 14:1-6; 1 Corinthians 9:20-21; 2 Corinthians 3:1-11; Galatians 3:3,11; Col. 2:16-17).

NOTES:

## Appendix 3

# Sample List of Unifying Values

1. ***We value the congregation, Matthew 16:18*** - Disciples of Yeshua in mutual and loving accountability in the Lord.

2. ***We value ministry by the fellowship, Ephesians 4:12*** - The Congregation Leader's ministry is to prepare the believers for service.

3. ***We value unity of faith, Amos 3:3*** - The Bible is the final authority; the Articles of Faith articulates our unity of beliefs.

4. ***We value diversity of service, 1 Peter 4:10-11; Luke 10:38-42*** - The congregation gives opportunity to each member for service. Counsel and encouragement for ministry is provided (priesthood of every believer).

5. ***We value leadership for effective ministry, Proverbs 29:18, 1 Timothy 3:5*** - A congregational ministry is established when a leader is raised up. We only do those ministries when we have the personnel to properly accomplish the service.

6. ***We value clarity and orderliness, 1 Corinthians 14:40*** - Life and love is not well expressed in chaos; communication is a priority (Constitution, bulletins, budgets, etc.).

7. ***We value the testimony of Messiah, Romans 1:16*** - We exalt His Name above all others. Evangelism and outreach is taught, conducted and encouraged.

8. ***We value a Messianic form of worship, Romans 11:1-2, 11-15, 17-24, 31*** - As Messianic Jews and Messianic Gentiles we express our faith in a Jewish cultural religious context (terminology, holidays, etc).

9. ***We value our kids, Psalm 127:3*** - The congregation provides instruction in the faith in a Jewish frame of reference.

10. ***We value discipleship, Matthew 28: 19-20*** - We have personal and group discipleship for all. Members are disciples.

NOTES:

## Appendix 4

# "How Are We Doing?"

Simple questions to evaluate a Messianic congregation's intentional progress: Faith is intentional trust and commitment (*kavanah)* to HaShem's calling and revealed word for us. For each of us to grow into Messiah, we must be faithfully committed to that purpose which He has for each of us, that is, "being conformity to the image of the Son" (Romans 8:29). The same is true of a congregation. The Messianic congregation will bring Him glory to the degree the community is revealing Yeshua. This also takes an intentional commitment in the areas of prayer, word (evangelism & discipleship) and overseer (servant leadership).

These next several evaluations are meant to assist the congregation and its leadership in further spiritual development into "the fullness and stature of the Son of God" (Ephesians 4:12-13).

Individual leaders can use these evaluation tools, however, they are meant for the whole leadership team to ascertain the congregation's strengths and areas for further ministry development. Eventually of course, this may impact the congregation's activities and therefore can be a tool for the whole of the membership to be able to utilize and develop each of their areas of service, as it "builds itself up in love" (Ephesians 4:15-16).

NOTES:

## 1. Intentional Evangelism: Making Contacts into Disciples

1. How much weekly prayer is there for this work in hours by people? ( 1 person 1 hour = 1 hour per week; 2 people 1 hour each = 2 hours per week)
2. How is training for outreach conducted and how often? How many classes are available in the year for training on evangelism? What books or websites are regularly recommended on evangelism? What percentage of members has been trained? (Give one for each yearly class; one for each book or website which is regularly recommended; one for each 10% of the congregation who have been trained)

3. How many activities and services are there to make contacts per week? (1 service once a week = 1; 1 service + 3 havurot, and 3 classes per week plus 1 team handing out tracts or going door to door = 8, etc.)

4. How many different leaders are involved in each of these activities? (1 person for 3 activities = 1; 3 people for 3 activities = 3; 3 people for three activities + 2 coordinator = 4, etc.; give + 1 point per leader if there is also an assistant that can stand in for the leader)

5. What means do you have to capture contacts' info? How effective are the activities? How do you know? Are there measurable results? How many people are there to follow up each week? (1 = 1, etc.)

6. How many people are there involved in the follow up each week (1 = 1, etc.)

## INTENTIONAL EVANGELISM EVALUATION

| Priority | 1-3 | 4-6 | 7-9 | 10-12 | 13-15 | 16-20 | Totals |
|---|---|---|---|---|---|---|---|
| Prayer | | | | | | | |
| Training | | | | | | | |
| Activities | | | | | | | |
| Leadership | | | | | | | |
| Contacts | | | | | | | |
| Follow up | | | | | | | |
| Totals | | | | | | | |

NOTES:

## INTENTIONAL EVANGELISM SCORING:

- 1-3, we're the "us four and no more crowd, and we want to keep it that way!" There needs to be retraining of the leadership to understand the congregational healthiness of outreach.
- 4-10, we're beginning to understand and apply the priority of outreach and evangelism! At the low end (4-6), there are not enough. More prayer etc. is needed to attain health. At the high end (7-10), this is a good start but be sure to give a vision of greater growth in outreach ministries.
- 11-30, we're healthy and very desirous to do more. Evangelism is in our DNA and we rejoice in this matter.
- 31-60, we're a mature congregation, which continues to train and seek to reach out even beyond our community.

- • 61-90, we're a sending and training center congregation, which helps other congregations in the work of ministry.

- • 91-100, who are we kidding, no one is that mature, and I better stop calling everything I do outreach, and every person I meet is both a contact and leader!

### IMPROVEMENT PLANNING FOR INTENTIONAL EVANGELISM

1. What 2-3 areas can you address in starting a planning process to improve this area of ministry? Areas:______________________________

2. Who else needs to be involved in the planning and the process?

Name______________________________________________

3. Whenwillyoustartthisprocess?Date__________________________

## 2. INTENTIONAL DISCIPLESHIP: MAKING DISCIPLES INTO MEMBERS

- How much weekly prayer is there for this discipleship ministry in hours by people? ( 1 person 1 hour = 1 hour per week; 2 people 1 hour each = 2 hours per week)

- What materials, activities are being used for this? How many materials are available for the different levels of discipleship and training for service? (1 =1)

- Do all potential members understand they are to participate in congregational service and ministry duties to maintain membership? Are all members discipled in the faith and have all agreed on the congregation's values? (For every 10% give yourself 1, with a possible total of 5)

- How many members are involved in discipling others? (1 =1; 1 discipling 2 = 2; but 1 person doing everything = 1)

- What various systems and activities are involved to get new members into service? ( Individual discipleship of 1 on 1 = 1 for each doing this activity, so 4 involved on 1 on 1 = 4; small groups and Shabbat school and other classes count as 1 each if they are intentionally making disciples.)

- Are there evaluations of their service? He often are the ministries and those involved evaluated? (Give 1 per month of review and evaluation, with a

NOTES:

possible total of 12; if there is training for reviews, give one per yearly training session; if there are more than 1 trainer, give each individual the 2nd and following 1 per)

- How many people who are discipled come into membership? (Give 1 per 1)
- What percentage of the active membership are involved in congregational activities and service? (1 per every 10%, with a possible score of 10)

## INTENTIONAL DISCIPLESHIP EVALUATION

| Priority | **1-3** | **4-10** | **11-40** | **41-60** | **61-80** | **101+** | **Totals** |
|---|---|---|---|---|---|---|---|
| Prayer | | | | | | | |
| Materials | | | | | | | |
| % Disciples | | | | | | | |
| Discipling | | | | | | | |
| Activities | | | | | | | |
| Evaluation | | | | | | | |
| Membership | | | | | | | |
| % Involved | | | | | | | |
| Totals | | | | | | | |

NOTES:

## INTENTIONAL DISCIPLESHIP SCORING

- 1-3, the lowest common denominator is our membership maturity goals and we want to keep it that way! There needs retraining of the leadership to understand the congregational healthiness of intentional discipleship.
- 4-10, we're beginning to understand and apply the priority of intentional discipleship! At the low end (4-6), there not enough and more prayer, etc is needed to attain health; at the high end (7-10), this is a good start but be sure to give a vision of greater growth in outreach ministries.
- 11-30, we're healthy and very desirous to do more; Discipleship is in our DNA and we rejoice in this matter.
- 31-60, we're a mature congregation, which continues to train and seek to disciple even beyond our community.
- 61-90, we're a discipleship training center congregation, which helps other congregations in the work of intentional discipleship ministry

- 91-100+, who are we kidding, no one is that mature, and I better stop calling everything I do as intentional discipleship, and every person I meet is both a disciple and trainer!

### IMPROVEMENT PLANNING FOR INTENTIONAL DISCIPLESHIP:

- What 2-3 areas can you address in starting a planning process to improve this area of ministry? Areas: __________ ____________________________
- Who else needs to be involved in the planning and the process?

Names: __________ ____________ ___________________________

- When will you start this process? Date_____________________________

## 3. INTENTIONAL LEADERSHIP DEVELOPMENT: MATURING MEMBERS INTO LEADERS

- How much weekly prayer is there for this leadership ministry and the leaders in hours by people? (1 person 1 hour = 1 hour per week; 2 people 1 hour each = 2 hours per week)
- Are members taking responsibility for the ministries of the congregation? (these may include elders and *shamashim* that are actually handling actual ministries) How many members are involved in handling the oversight of the regular activities and ministries in the congregation? (Give 1 for 1)
- Is there a process or program for developing members into leaders? Are there books recommended, classes available in the congregation, mentoring opportunities? Are there assistants to help train and be involved with each responsible leader who is able to handle the activity if the leader is not available? (Give 1 for each book regularly recommended; 1 for each regularly scheduled class per year; give 1 per assistant)
- What is your reporting system for assuring results match the plan? (Give 1 for each regularly scheduled meeting to report and evaluate the ministries and the results of the planned programs)

NOTES:

## INTENTIONAL LEADERSHIP EVALUATIONS

| Priorities | 1-3 | 4-10 | 11-25 | 26-50 | 51-100+ | Totals |
|---|---|---|---|---|---|---|
| Prayer | | | | | | |
| # Involved | | | | | | |
| Development | | | | | | |
| Reporting | | | | | | |
| Totals | | | | | | |

## INTENTIONAL LEADERSHIP SCORING:

- 1-3, I want to control all the power, and only have certain persons I fully trust to support me! There needs retraining of the leadership to understand the congregational healthiness of intentional leadership development.
- 4-10, we're beginning to understand and apply the priority of intentional leadership! At the low end (4-6), there is not enough happening and more prayer, etc. is needed to attain health; at the high end (7-10), this is a good start but be sure to give a vision of greater growth in leadership responsibility.
- 11-30, we're healthy and very desirous to do more; maturity into leadership is in our DNA and we rejoice in this matter.
- 31-60, we're a mature congregation, which continues to train and seek to develop leaders even beyond our own community.
- 61-90, we're a leadership training center congregation, which helps other congregations in the work of intentional leadership development
- 91-100+, who are we kidding, no one is that mature, and I better stop calling everything I do as intentional leadership training, and every person I meet both a leader!

NOTES:

______________________

______________________

______________________

______________________

______________________

______________________

______________________

______________________

______________________

______________________

## IMPROVEMENT PLANNING FOR INTENTIONAL LEADERSHIP DEVELOPMENT:

1. What 2-3 areas can you address and starting a planning process to improve this area of ministry? Areas: __________ _____________ _____

2. Who else needs to be involved in the planning and the process? Names: __________ ____________ __________ __________________ _

3. When will you start this process? Date______________________

## Appendix 5

# RECRUITMENT AND CARE FOR PEOPLE: A CHECKLIST

We recognize from Scripture that all leaders are responsible to be in prayer for the people and ministry in which they are involved. Also the ministry of the Word and its values needs to be expressed in their area of responsibility as well as overseeing (managing, caring for, shepherding, etc.) their specific area of involvement (Exodus 18; Acts 6, etc.).

A growing congregation is called to care for and help more and more people. Therefore, there needs to be a team approach which will not merely handle needs as they existed in the past, but as they will be in the future. In my experience it seems one of the most neglected yet vitally needed areas is the need for leaders to continue to grow in the area of the overseeing and recruitment.

If any of these matters are too much for a leader, there is no need for concern (we are all growing!). But I recommend they speak to those they report to for handling the responsibility.

## I. PREPARING TO RECRUIT

***A. Pray, think through and write down,*** "In light of the mission and values of the congregation, what part does my area of service play in fully accomplishing our mandate?" Write down the mission of your ministry within the congregation. This is your focus and content of service

1) In light of the mission you have just written down, consider the following questions:

- Am I clear on what is expected of me?
- How many more people are needed for the present work load?
- How many more people would be needed if the congregation grew by 50 people?
- Do other individuals need assistance?

2) Be clear on the requirements of various personnel for the team:
   - Are there special skills needed (technical, musical, oratory, relational, etc.)?
   - Are there unusual demands on time (will they miss a service, Shabbat school, have to come early, or stay late; attend rehearsals, etc.)?
   - Is there a need for special equipment, handling of funds, or interacting with people?

NOTES:

***B. Pray, think through and write an answer:*** "What are your present resources in people who are assisting you."

- Are they adequately trained and reliable in their responsibilities?
- Can they help train others to assist them?
- Is at least one of them trained to assist me in case I am away?

## II. PLANNING TO RECRUIT (TARP)

***A. Pray, think through, and write down,*** "How do I get from where I am now to where I want to be?"

Are the materials developed, which will help you to orient new people who will serve with you, as well as re-orient people already serving with you. This is so you will be ready to have people serve with you. To ascertain this readiness, ask yourself and note:

- Do I have a written job description for the various responsibilities?
- Is there a work schedule developed with regular team meetings planned into the schedule?
- Is there a step-by-step process to accomplish the tasks which needs to be provided?
- Am I ready to tell them what policy, procedures; ethical, legal, biblical, budgetary, concerns will be the boundaries of the responsibility?
- If this is not yet written down, how soon can I get this written down?
- Who can assist in this recruiting process?

NOTES:

***B. Am I ready to recruit people to serve?***

- What means will I use to recruit people? (i.e., email, bulletin, website, announcements, after service meeting, new members' class, etc)
- What info will you put in bulletin? Website? Flyer?
- Who will make the announcement? (preferably someone invested in this area of ministry)
- Am I ready to personally approach people and ask them to assist?
- Will I have a meeting to speak to interested people where I share the mission and vision, the victories experienced, the growth attained, blessings of service, etc? Can someone help me in this?

***C. Am I ready develop and care for others?***

1. Once they've agreed to help out and show themselves willing to follow direction, am I ready to clearly and directly orient them on the task (Eph 4:15-16)?

- How long will this stage take?
- Will I schedule time for myself or another to get them oriented?

- Will I go over the materials with them, walk them through, or have them watch me do it to make sure they understand and clarify what is being asked from them?
- What should be the result if this is properly accomplished?
- Is there an objective way to know if the responsibility was properly carried out?

2. Once they've been involved and are proven reliable, am I ready to patently and accurately answer their questions and explain the Biblical values behind the activities we're involved in?

- How can I be sure they grasp the values?
- Can they explain the values, procedures back to me?
- If I can't answer their questions, to whom I can send them to for answers?

3. Once they've grasped the values in their activities, am I ready to encourage them to participate in handling responsibilities and developing new and better or other ways within those responsibilities to accomplish the ministry mandate without changing the underlying values.

- Can this be done at a team meeting where you ask for new ideas, or note problems that need to be solved?
- How will it help more people? Will it minister to people not currently being helped?
- Will this need new programs or equipment?
- Will this call for additional personnel?
- Will it be accomplished sooner with the same budget and personnel? How will this impact budget?
- Will it need additional training?
- Can changes be made without hurting other ministry areas?
- Will you need to confer with other leaders to discuss potential impact on them?
- Will appear to conflict with the mission?
- Will a new approach need to be communicated to others, which may be impacted by this?

4. Once they've shown they can incorporate the values into new or other activities in their responsibilities, are you ready delegate to them authority and accountability in a position title that reflects the responsibilities they have?

- Will others on the team, other leaders, or members in the congregation realize the reasonableness of this delegation?
- Is approval acquired?
- How will that impact your responsibilities?

NOTES:

- How will it impact the rest of the team?
- How will it impact the goals for the team?
- Will this impact present reporting issues?

## III. IMPLEMENTING TO RECRUIT: PLAN

The plan should include who will be doing what by when on the matters noted above.

A. ***The plan should include who is expected to handle the particular responsibility***

- Have you reviewed your plan with anyone?
- All activities are handled by someone (team leaders); do you know who, and for what activity?
- Can this be developed and delegated at a team meeting?
- Does the team leader and members on the team know what each person is responsible to accomplish and within what period of time?
- Is there a reporting system, which will evaluate what is getting done?

***B. The plan should include what is to be accomplished.***

- Is it clear to the team, to you, and especially the team leader assigned to the task, what exactly needs to be done?
- Is the task specific enough?
- Is it part of the assigned team leader's regular responsibilities? If not, is it asking too much of them?
- Do they have the resources (money, equipment, info, etc) to do the task?
- Is there an objective result once it is accomplished?
- Are these specifics written down and available for review?

***C. The plan should include when the responsibility should be accomplished.***

- Has it been agreed to?
- Is it realistic if more training is needed?
- What if timing doesn't work out, can adjustments be made?
- How will you know when it is accomplished?

Remember, take everything one step at a time. Some steps will be easier than others. Some steps will need greater clarification and assistance than others, which is okay, and it is to be expected, even so let us press on to the mark of our high calling in Yeshua.

# Glossary of Messianic Jewish Terms

AM HA-ARETZ ("people of the land"): common people, later used in the Talmud to refer to uneducated, unobservant Jews

AMIDAH ("standing"): also called the *Shmoneh Esrei* ("eighteen") because of its eighteen blessings originally composed probably both before and after the destruction of the Temple (70CE). It is also considered central Jewish prayer.

AVODAH ("worship"): service to God, originally applied to Temple service. Literally means "work."

BEIT TEFILAH ("House of Prayer"): Originally referring to the Temple, a prayer and worship center (Isaiah 56:7).

BEMA ("high place"): pulpit or raised platform

BESORAH ("Message"): the Good News, or Gospel

BIRKAT HACOHANIM ("The Blessing of the Priests"): Aaronic Benediction, taken from Numbers 6:24-26

BRIT CHADASHAH (also *habrit hachadasha*, "New Covenant"): the Apostolic Writings, often called the "New Testament." The term is from Jeremiah 31:31.

BRIT MILAH ("covenant of circumcision"): ceremony of circumcision performed upon Jewish males on the eighth day. Traditionally performed by a mohel. This ceremony is also called a bris.

CHAGIGAH means "Festival Sacrifice."

GEMARA ("completion"): the final layer of commentary of the Talmud, commenting on the Mishnah, compiled up to 500 CE.

HAGGADAH (also *aggadah*, pl. *haggadot*, "telling"): a booklet used to go through a Passover Seder, such as The Messianic Passover Haggadah. Also may refer to sections of Talmud and Midrash containing homiletic expositions of Bible, legends, and stories from tradition.

HALAKHA ("walking"): Traditional Jewish law, the expression of Torah in daily life and conduct.

HANUKKAH ("dedication"): Feast commemorating the rebuilding and dedication of the Temple after its desecration by Syrian invaders. Referenced in the books of extra-Biblical books of Maccabees and in John 10:22. From the verb hanakh or "train," used for a disciple.

HASHEM ("the Name"): a reverent and traditional way of referring to God. It refers specifically to his four-letter Personal Name, rendered in many English Bibles as "Lord," called the "tetragrammaton."

HAVURAH ("a fellowship"): a small group or Bible Study.

HAVERUT ("fellowship"): the sharing in what is common to a group a believers.

KAVANAH ("intentionality"): a traditional concept regarding how one is to pray to God. It speaks of being focused and not distracted; purposeful and not haphazard; fervent and not apathetic; reverent and not insolent.

KETUVIM ("Writings"): the third section of the Hebrew Bible (after Torah and Nevi'im).

KOHELET ("Preacher"): the main speaker of the Book of Ecclesiastes, as well as the Hebrew name of that book.

KOHEN GADOL ("High Priest")

MAIMONIDES: Rabbi Moshe ben Maimon (traditionally called by the acrostic "the RaMbaM"), the renowned Jewish teacher, philosopher, and physician, 1135-1204 CE.

MASHIACH ("Anointed," Greek *Christos* or "Christ"): Messiah, the Anointed of God to bring salvation to humanity.

MESSIANIC: a follower of Yeshua the Messiah, or a group of such followers. It differs from "Christian" in that it suggests a re-emphasis on the faithfulness of God, found in the Messiah, first to His people Israel and equally to all the Nations.

MINYAN (lit. "to count"): traditionally a quorum of ten men which is required for a corporate prayer service; informally, the prayer service itself.

MISHNAH ("repetition"): Legal codification of basic Jewish Law, and foundational to later Rabbinic Judaism. Compiled by Judah Ha-Nasi around 200CE. With Gemara, it makes up the Talmud.

NEVI'IM ("prophets"): the second of three sections of the Hebrew Bible, falling between Torah and Ketuvim.

OLAM HABA ("the world to come")

ONEG ("delight"): a time of refreshment with food after Shabbat services (oneg Shabbat can refer more broadly to various activities to enjoy Shabbat)

PASSOVER (Hebrew, *Pesach*): Foundational biblical holiday commemorating the rescue of the children of Israel from Egypt, and pointing to the sacrificial death of Messiah.

PURIM ("lots"): Holiday based on the book of Esther, often celebrated by giving gifts, dressing in costumes, and a dramatic reenactment of the story (a Purim play).

RASHI: Rabbi Shlomo Yitzchaki, famous for his foundational Rabbinic exegesis, 1040-1105CE.

ROSH HASHANAH ("head of the year"): Traditional Jewish New Year stemming from the Feast of Trumpets in Leviticus 23. See also Yom Teruah.

RUACH HAKODESH ("the Holy Spirit"): the Person Who is God and applies God's plan of redemption to the life of the believer. See Lessons 11 and 12. (Ruach = Spirit, breath, or wind)

SEDER ("order"): a structured meal celebrated usually on one of the first two nights of Passover. See The Messianic Passover Haggadah.

SHAMASH ("servant" or "deacon"): a level of servant-leadership found in Messianic congregations which is responsible for executing responsibilities within the congregation (see also *zaken*)

SHALIACH ("apostle," pl. *shlichim*).

SHAVUOT ("weeks," in Greek, Pentecost): Holiday known as the "Season of the Giving of the Law," also when the spirit of God was given to believers in Yeshua.

SHEMA ("Hear"): the centerpiece of Jewish liturgy, reciting Deuteronomy 6:4 and several additional passages.

SUKKOT ("booths," plural of *sukkah*): Feast to remember God's provision and protection in the wilderness wanderings, celebrated by creating and living in makeshift dwellings for eight days.

TALLIT (lit. "cloak"): prayer shawl with tzitzit traditionally worn at morning services and certain special times.

TALMID (lit. "student," pl. *talmidim*): a trained disciple.

TALMIDUT ("discipleship"): the process of becoming a *talmid* (student or disciple). A similar concept, *hanukkah,* from *hanakh*, connotes "training" or "dedication."

TALMUD ("study"): The primary written corpus of the "Oral Law." Made up of Mishnah and Gemara, there is both a Babylonian and Jerusalem Talmud, with the Babylonian Talmud being much larger and carrying more authority. Compiled from 200-500CE.

TANAKH: The Hebrew Bible, coming from an acrostic of its parts: Torah (Pentateuch), Nevi'im, and Ketuvim (Writings).

TEVILAH ("immersion"): the practice of plunging believers into water as a symbolic testimony of their identification with Messiah. Also called mikveh ("reservoir" or "collected water"), which refered to ceremonial cleansing for ritual purification, and thus became a word often used by believers to refer to immersion.

TORAH ("instruction"): Divine Instruction, the Scriptures. Also refers to the Five Books of Moses (or Pentateuch), and sometimes called the Law, due to appearance of Mosaic laws in this portion of the Hebrew Bible.

TZITZIT ("fringes"): knotted ritual fringes traditionally worn in obedience to the command in Numbers 15:38 and elsewhere.

YESHUA ("the Lord is salvation"): the Hebrew name often transliterated through the Greek as "Jesus," meaning "the Lord is salvation," or "the Lord saves."

YOM TERUAH ("day of blasting," or the Feast of Trumpets): A mysterious holiday found in Leviticus 23:24, this day begins the High Holy Days and Fall Feasts, and prophetically points to the catching up (or "rapture") of believers.

YOM KIPPUR ("day of atonement"): found in Leviticus 23:27-32, and simply called "the fast" in Acts 27:9, this close of the High Holy Days is considered the holiest day of the year in traditional Judaism. It points to the time of Israel's national repentance to Messiah (Zechariah 12:10).

ZAKEN ("elder"): the highest level of servant-leadership within the congregation, responsible for overseeing the teaching, preaching, prayer, worship, and administration of the congregation.

# Other Books and Materials by Sam Nadler

***Even You Can Share The Jewish Messiah*** - a short booklet with key information on sharing Yeshua with friends and neighbors, even "to the Jew first" (Romans 1:16).

***Messianic Foundations: Fulfill Your Calling in the Jewish Messiah*** - offers a vision of the Messianic Movement motivated by the testimony that Yeshua is God's faithfulness to Israel.

***The Messianic Answer Book*** - answers to the 15 most asked questions Jewish people have about the faith. Excellent tool for sharing with those seeking answers.

***Messiah in the Feasts of Israel*** - From Passover to Booths in the Torah, or Hanukkah and Purim in the Prophets and Writings, this book will deepen your understanding of the prophetic purpose of the Feasts; how they point us to Yeshua, and much more.

***The Messianic Passover Haggadah*** - the perfect guide for conducting your own Passover Seder.

***Messianic Discipleship: Following Yeshua, Growing in Messiah*** - leads the reader through a Jewish discipleship course, dealing with the essentials of Messianic faith.

***Messianic Wisdom: Practical Scriptural Answers for Your Life*** - get a grasp on Messianic Jewish issues and living out your faith in Messiah. Essential and inspiring, this book is for every growing disciple of Yeshua.

***Messianic Life Lessons from the Book of Ruth*** - an in-depth, information-rich devotional commentary on this priceless book of restoration from the Tanakh.

***Messianic Life Lessons from the Book of Jonah*** - do you want to know God's will for your life? Jonah proves that this alone will not help! A slender commentary on this book about Israel's mission to the Gentiles.

---

www.Messianicleadership.com - Word of Messiah's special web resource designed for Messianic congregational leaders and planters. View video podcasts, retrieve further notes, and other materials related to this book.

*To schedule Sam or receive more information, contact us:*


Word of Messiah Ministries

P.O. Box 79238

Charlotte, NC

28271, USA

Email: info@wordofmessiah.org

Phone: (704) 544-1948


Visit our website at:

WWW.WORDOFMESSIAH.ORG
WWW.MESSIANICLEADERSHIP.COM


*"Establishing Healthy Messianic Congregations: Planters, Planting, and Planning"*
*by Sam Nadler*



*Word of Messiah Ministries*



*Printed in the United States of America*
*ISBN 978-0-9786568-5-0*